Stronger Than a Speeding Bullet

GABRIEL TUGGLE

Stronger Than a Speeding Bullet
Copyright © 2022 by Gabriel Tuggle
Developmental Editor: Vivien Cooper

All rights reserved. No part of this publication
may be reproduced, distributed, or transmitted
in any form or by any means, including
photocopying, recording, or other electronic
or mechanical methods, without the prior
written permission of the author, except
in the case of brief quotations embodied
in critical reviews and certain other non-
commercial uses permitted by copyright law.

Tellwell Talent
www.tellwell.ca

ISBN
978-0-2288-7556-7 (Hardcover)
978-0-2288-7555-0 (Paperback)
978-0-2288-7557-4 (eBook)

*Dedicated to my mother,
the most important, amazing, awesome,
incredible woman in my life. She is my number-one fan,
and has stuck by me and been there for me through it all.
She is still sticking by me and believing in me.
Words cannot describe or explain how much
I LOVE YOU, Mom!
You are my Superwoman.*

Preface

I was born twice—first as a baby boy, on a crisp morning in Covington, Georgia on May 4th, 1972. Then again as a teenage boy on February 10th, 1991. My second birth took place in the operating room at Piedmont Hospital in Atlanta. That moment followed the shooting—one of the worst nightmares of my life. The fact that I am alive, healthy, and strong enough to tell you this story is a testament to the power of God.

It is written in the Bible book of Jeremiah, chapter 1, verse 5: *Before I formed you in the womb, I knew you. Before you were born, I set you apart for my holy purpose. I appointed you to be a prophet to the nations.*

God created me unique and perfect in His own image, with a holy purpose. But the road I took would end up causing pain not only for me but for those I love.

What you are about to read is the story of my trial, my pain, my triumph, and my joy. It is not a perfect story as I am not a perfect man. But I have come to realize that every disappointment, every decision, every struggle in my life has brought me to this part of the journey where I am able to share my life story with you.

My story may not be your story—but we all have a story about the life we've made it through. Each of our stories has something different and unique. By the time you reach the end of this book, I think you will agree that this is one of those stories that is especially different and unique. It is definitely not the sort of story you hear on a daily basis.

In these pages, you will witness God performing miracles—just like the many miracles He still performs to this day. It is my hope and prayer that as you read these pages, you will find the strength, hope, faith, and encouragement you need to keep going, keep fighting, and continue moving forward, knowing that you can overcome any obstacle you face.

With God, all things are possible.

One

On February 10th, 1991, I walked up to the house of a guy I'll call Spanky. That date would be forever burned in my mind. It was the day that changed my life—the day when everything I had worked so hard for, strived for, planned for, and fought for was snatched from me in a flash. I thought that day would be my last.

Spanky was one of the guys in the hip-hop dance group I had joined. His house was a big hangout spot for those of us in the group, and friends from the neighborhood too. Once I was inside the house, I could hear that everyone was hanging out in the back room, so I headed in there.

The guys were joking around, and I joined in the fun. I was happy being with them and having a good time. All I remember is that everyone was giving each other a hard time—but all the teasing was done in good fun. I made a remark to Spanky in that same spirit of fun. It was meant to be funny. I felt comfortable joking with him because I was among friends.

When they heard the funny thing I'd said, everyone in the room busted out laughing—everyone but Spanky. In that very moment, he happened to be cleaning his

Smith & Wesson .44, one of the most powerful handguns in the world.

I knew that he carried a bag with a gun in it, just in case someone started trouble. Our group was often in neighborhoods that weren't the best, and he thought he might one day need to use it in self-defense.

I could see a bunch of bullets on the bed. I assumed that he had removed all the bullets from the gun. To this day, I still don't know whether Spanky knew that one bullet was still in the chamber.

"What did you say, motherfu****?" He pointed the gun directly at me. His response to my teasing remark would be the last words I heard before becoming the miracle I am today.

Spanky shot me at point-blank range. There I was, with the brass ring within reach—and then that shot rang out. Now, I lay on the floor in a puddle of my own blood, helpless, with my life endangered due to a gunshot wound to the head.

In a split second, I died to all the hard work I had done in my efforts to set my mom free. I was considered a very promising athlete with a great future ahead of me. I could have written my ticket to play college football anywhere in the country—and I believe I could have gone on to play professional football or baseball.

My brother was there that day. He later told me that everyone in the room was running around like crazy, freaking out. Someone ran down the street to our house and told my mom, and someone else called an ambulance.

I was rushed to the local hospital by ambulance. They were not equipped to handle the level of brain swelling I was experiencing, so I was rushed from there to Piedmont Hospital in Georgia.

I was immediately prepped and taken into surgery. I stayed under the knife for several hours. I later found out that family members, classmates, teammates, and friends were calling. Everyone was scared and worried and wanted to find out how I was doing.

After many hours of surgery, my neurosurgeon, Dr. Gary Gropper, came out to deliver the sad news to my mom and brother-in-law, Neal Banks.

He said, "I'm sorry to tell you this, but the damage to Lamar's brain is severe. We are doing all we can for him, but he is likely to be in a vegetative state when he wakes up. He's probably going to have limited functionality for the rest of his life."

(At that point in life, I was called by my middle name, Lamar. Later in life, I would begin to call myself by my first name, Gabriel.)

My mother had to listen to the surgeon tell her that her youngest child, her baby boy, would never be normal. I was being written off. Little did she know that as Dr. Gropper was talking to her and my brother-in-law, and releasing me from his hands, God was stepping in and taking me into His hands!

Having no way of knowing that God had a miracle in store for me, my mother got incredibly upset over this terrible news. So did my entire family.

As Dr. Gropper returned to the operating room to finish surgery on me, Dr. God—the doctor who created both me and the surgeon—kept up His work, as well. He worked through the surgeon and used his hands to start building, shaping, and molding the clay (me) back together.

This Bible scripture, written in conversation form in the book of Ezekiel 37:3—6, fits my situation to a tee:

> *The Lord God asked me, "Son of man, can these bones live?"*
>
> *I said, "Sovereign Lord, you alone know."*
>
> *Then he said to me, "Prophesy to these bones and say to them, 'Dry bones, hear the words of the Lord! This is what the Sovereign Lord says to the bones: I will make breath enter you, and you will come to life. I will attach tendons to you and make flesh come upon you and cover you with skin; I will put breath in you, and you will come to life. Then you will know that I am the Lord."*

Along with my mother and grandmother, there were many, many people praying for me. God heard their prayers and performed a miracle, restoring me to wholeness.

God had spoken new life into me, and Dr. Gropper was amazed. While I was in the ICU being given special care by the hospital's best staff, I slowly started to regain consciousness.

When I was finally able to open my eyes, I was in unfamiliar territory. I saw three T.V.s on the wall. I was so drugged up from the medications they had me on, I had to close one eye just to see the one in the middle. I found myself in a very strange situation.

After about a week, I was moved out of ICU and into a private room on a special floor of the hospital. The doctors felt that I was likely to have seizures, so they kept a close eye on me to monitor my brain swelling. The swelling was giving me brutal migraine headaches.

Every so often throughout the day, nurses came in to take my blood, check my blood pressure, and give me medications. Others came by too. Now that I was out of ICU and in a private room, my visitors were no longer limited to family. My teachers, friends, and fellow students all came to visit me. So did my coaches and teammates from both football and baseball.

I was suffering from traumatic brain injury, so I didn't recognize anyone. Even members of my own family were like total strangers to me at the time. I can't imagine how scary that must have been for everyone, to see me act that way towards them. I just lay there and stared off into space.

I heard one of my visitors telling me, "You can't leave us! We need you back out on the baseball field!"

Later, one of my teammates from baseball told me that he was the one who had said that to me. I still couldn't speak at all, so I was unable to respond to anyone. All I could do was blink my eyes.

It was so painful to be lying there helpless, unable to respond, unable to do anything but listen and stare, with tears rolling down my face. I wasn't crying because I was an athlete whose sports career had been snatched from me by a bullet. I didn't yet recall any details of what had happened to me, or what I or my life had been like before the accident. All I knew was that something bad had happened.

Dr. Gropper came into the room and told my mom what to expect. "Lamar's going to be here for a while. He's got a long road ahead of him and he's going to have to fight for his recovery."

He explained that I was like a newborn baby, and I would have to relearn all the things I had already mastered in my former life. I had faced tough challenges before but this was a whole different ballgame.

Regaining the ability to walk, talk, respond, and interact was going to be the toughest challenge I would ever face in my life. It would take all my strength, might, and will. My life was definitely worth fighting for, but there was no question about it—it would be the fight of my life.

I had no idea how I was going to get back to a place of restored health and strength, but I was determined to figure it out. I was no stranger to hard work. I was used to putting in the kind of effort needed to excel in sports.

Somehow, I knew I was up for the challenge, even if I didn't yet remember the challenges I had already overcome in my life.

Two

Dr. Gropper and his staff came into my room and handed me a mirror so they could show me the large staples they had used to close the surgical wound. When I saw my head, I couldn't believe my eyes. I felt like I was in a horror movie. I looked like a victim of Jason, the character from the *Friday the 13th* movies. It looked like I had been attacked with an axe…or a chainsaw!

In addition to having nursing staff come into my room every so often, I also had to go down to radiology once or twice a week for CT scans of my brain. After a few weeks, I began regaining my memory. I was seriously grateful for this and happy to see how happy it made my family and loved ones when I recognized them.

During the entire time I remained in the hospital, people kept coming to visit me. One person was noticeably absent—the guy who had shot me and forever changed my life! He didn't come to see me at any point while I was hospitalized.

I was disturbed by the fact that Spanky never even came by to check on me. To this day, I still don't understand why he didn't come to the hospital to see how I was doing, or to my house once I was released. In any case, I knew I couldn't let it bother me too much. I couldn't afford to get discouraged while I was fighting for my survival and on a mission to get my normal life back.

I can't remember whether my family ever talked about going after Spanky legally. I do know that no legal action was ever taken. The people who were present in the room during the shooting, and the neighborhood kids, all referred to the shooting as an accident. I don't know why. He pointed the gun directly at me.

It had only been about a month since I'd been shot and already the healing process was underway. But I was still so weak. The power and impact of the gunshot, and the fact that I was shot at point-blank range, had made my head and neck snap really hard. It weakened the bones in my neck so much that I could barely hold my head up. That was another battle I had to overcome.

It was time for me to start physical therapy and speech therapy so I could relearn how to walk, talk, and feed myself. Soon, I started walking a little bit, very slowly. And after being unable to talk at all, I was soon able to moan and to slowly, carefully nod or shake my head when spoken to or asked a question.

The doctors and nurses were amazed and impressed with my progress. All of this was way ahead of schedule. It was very rare to have survived a point-blank gunshot wound to the head and be coming along so well.

I still had a long way to go. It was so difficult to accept that I—the same kid who used to get in trouble for talking so much in class!—was still unable to form words.

As I continued to fight daily for my recovery, the doctors, nurses, and therapists saw that I was a strong and willing individual.

I knew that all the work I had put in to become the best football and baseball player I could be was serving me well in this situation. That same determination and work ethic carried over into me working extra hard and going the extra mile. Now, I was fighting for something way more important than sports—my life!

I am not someone to ever quit or give up. God instilled in me the will to persevere, and I fought like I had never fought before. Just like my teammates and sports coaches had seen how hard I was willing to work to become the best player I could be, the doctors and nurses were seeing the same thing in the way I fought for my recovery.

My determination was obvious. The doctors and nurses were always telling me and my family that they had never seen anyone before me bounce back so quickly or respond so well to treatment.

Even though I was happy to be progressing so well with my healing, it was very frustrating to be unable to do basic things on my own. I took my encouragement from the good results that I got from my CT scans and my daily rehab.

I pushed myself to walk farther than the nurses expected me to, with some assistance from my family members. Every time I could see myself making progress, I used that as my motivation and slowly rebuilt my confidence. I still wasn't able to talk very well.

Going into month two of my recovery in the hospital, I realized that I was getting a little stronger and walking better. Little by little, I was also slowly relearning to feed myself. I still needed help, but I was making progress in that area. These little wins kept my hopes alive.

I thought of being a little boy and attending vacation Bible school during the summertime. One of my favorite scriptures was Matthew 19:26, which states: *"With man, this is impossible but with God, all things are possible."*

I also thought of a story the teacher used to read aloud to us in school when I was little: *The Little Engine That Could*. As the little red engine kept chugging up the hill, he was chanting to himself, *I think I can, I think I can.*

When he realized that he could make it to the top, his confidence grew, and his self-talk became more positive. He started chanting, *I know I can, I know I can!*

Just like the little red engine that could, I too started shifting into positive-thinking mode. I realized that my faith was being tested. I was going through something most people never have to go through, and I had to figure out a way to get through it and come out strong and healed on the other side.

No one in the hospital could understand how I was managing to get better, and they were astounded by my progress. There was something living on the inside of me that was allowing me to keep going, something pushing me to fight and not give up.

The big lesson I was having to learn was that I was not in control of my recovery. Yes, I was pushing through and getting better, little by little—but to some extent, the results of my efforts were out of my hands.

This wasn't like sports, where the more effort and work I put in, the better the results. I was doing what I could on my end to heal and get better, but God was also working on my healing. I wasn't in charge of His work, His plan, His timing for my recovery, or His will for my body and my life.

The doctors and nurses were still keeping a close eye on me. Because I had suffered a serious brain injury, the doctors felt that there was a strong possibility of me experiencing seizures. They went so far as to tell me to expect to have seizures! Thankfully, I never did.

I was coming up on my third month in the hospital. I would go downstairs for daily rehab and then come back up to my room.

I was getting better and a little bit stronger in terms of walking and feeding myself. I was even starting to talk a little bit. When someone spoke to me, I could respond in a very basic way. My words were slurred but everyone understood what I was saying.

By this point in my recovery, my daily tests were coming back looking good. My final CT scan also looked promising. So, the doctors and nurses decided to release me and allow me to go home. Going home proved to be a real test of my commitment to my recovery. It also tested my faith and my belief that everything was happening in God's way and in His divine timing.

As he released me from the hospital, Dr. Gropper explained to my mom how imperative it was that I continue my regular check-ups with him and return to the hospital three times a week for my rehab treatments. He gave Mom the playbook for my recovery and instructions on how to execute it. He let her know that if we followed it and stuck with it, I should be fine.

I was leaving the hospital in a wheelchair, after spending a little over two months there. As the nurse pushed my wheelchair, other nurses and doctors were watching in amazement. Everyone started applauding.

They knew that they were watching a miracle patient leave the hospital, and they were astounded. None of the medical personnel had thought I would go on to live a normal life, due to my brain damage being so severe. The nurse pushing my wheelchair told me what a fighter I was, and she encouraged me to stay strong and keep fighting for my full recovery.

My physical therapy and speech therapy sessions did not address my emotional trauma. I may have had one or two sessions with a mental health professional to deal with the trauma, but nothing on an ongoing basis. Since I never had ongoing, structured mental-health therapy, I left the hospital with underlying trauma.

From time to time, a wave of trauma would still come up. (Waves of trauma still occasionally come up, even to this day.) Later when I was healed enough to have my own apartment, I would sit on my bed, looking at the get-well cards and photos of me playing football, and tears would flow. I recently told my sister how heavy that was for me.

I was so blessed to have a large portion of my medical bills paid by the health insurance through my mom's work. (At the time of the shooting, I was still on her policy.)

Unfortunately, we ended up with a mountain of medical bills anyway. The insurance didn't cover them completely. Mom did her best to pay the bills little by little, over time, as she was able to. Bill collectors got inpatient with the pace at which she was paying them back, and they came after her and garnished her wages.

Before the accident, I had been super close to being able to play pro ball and finally reach my goal of freeing my mother financially—and instead, she ended up getting stuck with all these medical bills on my behalf. It wasn't my fault, but it hurt anyway.

Once I was well enough to work again, I slowly paid her back. It took me two or three years to completely repay her. I believe that, at some point while we are both on this earth, I will be taking care of her. In the meantime, God is taking care of her.

Three

I have three siblings. My sister Pam is four years older than me, and she is the oldest of us four. Then came my brother, Dexter, and my sister Monica.

Then, on the 4th day of May in 1972, God would bless our mother with her final child—a fourth angel she would name Gabriel Lamar. I would bring her great joy. My mother felt that there was something special about me, her last baby boy.

In that time period of the 1960s and '70s in rural Georgia, there was racism and other obstacles that were not only challenging but potentially dangerous. Unfortunately, after the death of Martin Luther King, Jr. in 1968, the civil rights movement slowed considerably and was no longer at the forefront of the news.

After the enormous struggle for equality by our people, the nation's priorities shifted. It was now about the healing of a broken nation. The land of the free, home of the brave had to take a hard look in the mirror. It was time to be brutally honest and admit that it had not given equal rights to all its citizens. Covington, Georgia was certainly not a place that gave its citizens the equal rights they deserved.

As recently as 2015, Pope Francis visited the White House and acknowledged this lack of equality before both Democrats and Republicans in Congress. He pointed out to America that they had not been fair to everyone. They had not done enough.

On a daily basis, we Black Americans in Covington were spoken to in a way that was disrespectful and demeaning. We continued to struggle for acknowledgement and respect. We were fed the same white supremacy message which continues to isolate us in today's world.

Racism continued in Covington until Tyrone Brooks, Rev. Hosea Williams, and Rev. Dr. Ralph Abernathy—some of Martin Luther King, Jr.'s major players—came down from Atlanta. When they arrived, they continued to march and fight for us Black Americans.

Seeing such leaders of prominence championing our cause was exciting and motivating. But it wouldn't be until 1977 that Covington finally had its first Black American politician—county commissioner, Harold Cobb.

Two years later, we got a second Black American politician, City Councilman, Eddie Baker. And, in 1983, a Black American woman, Janet Goodman, joined the City Council. In 2008, we got our first Black American sheriff—Ezell Brown. He had worked in law enforcement for thirty-five years prior to becoming sheriff.

Getting these Black American politicians in Covington was a beacon of light in an otherwise bleak landscape for the Black residents of our town. It was like getting a jumpstart off the starting block of the race—just like John Baxter Taylor Jr., the first Black American to win the gold medal in track-and-field in 1908. That win was around the time Black Americans started getting recognized for their accomplishments and excellence.

Certain moments in history give us hope that we might have an even playing field—like when Jackie Robinson became the first Black American to play baseball in the major leagues, and when three-time All American, Ernie Davis, became the first Black American to win the Heisman Trophy.

Those were significant accomplishments and strides, yet the challenges and struggles for African Americans in this country persist to this day. Despite all the turmoil and upheaval plaguing our nation, my mother successfully raised four children on her own.

Unfortunately, Mom was a victim of severe domestic violence. She suffered at the hands of her very abusive husband until her parents and her sister came to our rescue and removed us from the household. Mom now became a single mother. Dad was out of the picture.

My mother wasn't the only woman suffering abuse. Domestic abuse of Black American women was one of the prominent issues of that time period. This issue was swept under the rug due to rampant racism. Sadly, very little has changed, even to this day.

Mom knew it would be hard being a single mother of four kids. She also knew that she had no choice but to leave. Had we stayed in that environment with our father, the outcome could have been devastating. I was still a baby at the time, so I had very little memory of my father. But as I grew up, I would hear stories of how he abused my mother.

My grandparents—who everyone called Big Mama and Big Daddy—took us to their house and moved us in with them. We would stay there until my mother could earn the money to get us our own place. Things were very difficult for Mom. Not only did her marriage fall apart but she had to put an extra burden on her parents by moving herself and us four kids into their home.

They had a two-bedroom, one-bath house. Their sons, Uncle Jerry and Uncle Charles, lived there with them. Their two daughters, Aunt Gracie and Aunt Barbara, and their families lived right down the street, next door to each other.

In addition to their children, my grandparents also had chickens, ducks, and a garden that my grandfather tended every morning before he went into work. Living with my grandparents was like living on Old MacDonald's farm from the children's nursery rhyme. *Old MacDonald had a farm, ee-i-ee-i-o...and on his farm he had some chicks...*

Between my grandparents, their two sons, my mother, and us four kids, we had one big, blended family that filled up every space in the house. It was difficult living in such close quarters. Mom was determined to give us kids love and a sense of normalcy, even in that tight situation.

Looking back on it as an adult, I'm very grateful to my grandparents for taking us in and making room for us. It was better to live jammed in together in a loving household than it would have been living one more day in that hostile, violent situation that could have potentially ended all our lives.

It was my grandparents, our guardian angels, who gave us a fighting chance to make a difference in this world. Our family was like Mary and Joseph, looking for a place to lay their heads in Bethlehem. We each had to find a comfortable place to sleep in my grandparents' crowded house.

With so many people jammed in together, it wasn't easy to find a little square of the house that wasn't already occupied. (My mom may have been sleeping on the living room couch. It's hard to recall.)

There was space on the floor in the living room, but all my grandparents could offer us in the way of comfort was some extra blankets to help soften up the hardness of the floor. At the age of three when I was old enough to sleep on my own, I slept on a small pallet made of blankets, right next to a gas heater.

I was too young to know it was dangerous to sleep so close to a heater. All I knew was that the heat felt good on those cold winter nights in Covington. In the wintertime, the cold wind came in under the doors. It also found its way inside from the windows. My grandfather covered the windows with plastic and put towels and blankets up against the bottoms of the doors. We did whatever we could to keep warm.

Then there were the mice which ran freely at night, and the roaches which made themselves at home in the dark but scattered when we switched on a light. God's grace and mercy were with us. He kept us safe and protected during those trying times.

Big Daddy had an impeccable work ethic. As the patriarch in the family, my grandfather was the one setting the standard and showing the rest of us in the household how to be responsible and successful. Every morning when he got up to do his chores, he was showing us the importance of avoiding laziness.

I watched Big Daddy teaching my uncles how to tend to the animals and look after the garden. I saw how quickly he went about doing his chores before work. He also taught my brother, who wanted to help out before he went to school.

The decades of sacrifice, hard work, and grind started to take their toll on my grandfather's health. When I was only four years old, Big Daddy began to experience aches and pains in his legs. Each day, it got a little worse. Finally, he went to the doctor to find out what was causing the pain.

The doctor told him that he had high cholesterol and a serious vascular condition. As a result of my grandfather's vascular issues, both of his legs had to be amputated. This was devastating news and a tragic outcome for a man who had once been a man's man, a hero.

Every morning after working the nightshift, Mom would come home, take a little nap, pick me up from pre-K, and then drive an hour each way to Georgia Baptist Hospital in Atlanta to visit my grandfather.

I went with her to the hospital nearly every day. Getting to see my grandfather so often was a wonderful, heartwarming gift. I loved to sit and listen to his words of wisdom. At four years old, I had no idea that the words he was speaking to me then would hold true for me now.

Between going back and forth to the hospital to see my grandfather, working, and taking care of us kids, Mom was running around like a chicken with her head cut off. It was a lot for her to handle but she was making it happen. That wasn't unusual for my mom. She often made major sacrifices for us kids. Sometimes she went without, just so we could have what we needed.

A mother's love is limitless. It enables her to support her children in so many ways. A mother is a protector, a disciplinarian, and a friend. A mother is a selfless, loving person who must sacrifice many of her wants and needs for the wants and needs of her children. A mother works hard to make sure her children are equipped with the traits, knowledge, skills, and abilities they need in order to make it as competent human beings.

Being a mother is one of the hardest, most rewarding jobs a woman can experience. Mothers are examples of true, unconditional LOVE. That's why I called our mother Supermom. (I still do!) She was the backbone for the four of us kids. She always went beyond her responsibilities to us.

With both of his legs now amputated, Big Daddy was no longer able to do many of the things he once took for granted. Once his stumps healed from the surgery, he had to get two wooden prosthetic legs. He learned how to walk on them—but it was impossible for him to provide for his family anymore.

The same man who had been a father figure to the four of us now found himself depending on his family because he could no longer do the things he once did. This was a hard reality for my grandfather to swallow.

Thank God for strong men in my bloodline. My uncles stepped up to the plate and made sure all the work was done. They had done this while my grandfather was in the hospital, preparing for the fight of his life, and they kept it up after he got home. Uncle Charles was a house painter. Uncle Jerry worked at Covington Molding, the local molding factory, after he graduated from high school. Big Mama worked there too.

My mother also pitched in, working even harder to help with the household expenses. She worked at MacGregor (a manufacturer of golf balls), and at a later point in time, she worked as a nurse. Mom did whatever she could to help.

Seeing Big Daddy go through this terrible situation when I was so young motivated me to do some research later in life. I was determined to find out how to remain in the best health and shape possible. This commitment to my health and fitness paid off when I later established myself in football.

Thankfully, I come from strong stock. I am descended from an amazing warrior. And, as we all know, behind any great warrior, there must be a strong woman who stands by his side and has his back. That woman was my grandmother. She was the one who kept the show going without skipping a beat.

Big Mama had a crazy amount of faith. She wholeheartedly trusted and believed in Big Daddy's vision for our family, and she made sure it didn't fall by the wayside when he could no longer provide for us. She made sure that we carried my grandfather's vision forward into our lives—learning how to become providers, keeping a strong work ethic, and holding onto the same family values he had always exemplified.

Four

Ever since I was two or three, Mom had seen how excited I got every time I ran and picked up a football. She saw what great joy it brought me to put my hands on a football and play with it. She also recognized how excited I got every time we went to see my brother, Dexter, play his sports.

As I got older, I started watching Dexter play rec football. Seeing my brother play football really amplified my interest in the game. I loved how quick he was and how he was able to elude players on the opposite team when they tried to tackle him. I learned some of those techniques from my brother and used them myself later on when I was on a team.

Dexter had already been playing football for a year or so by the time I was old enough to start elementary school. The following year, when it came time to sign my brother up for football again, Mom signed me up too. At the same time, she signed my sisters up for cheerleading.

I don't know where Mom got the money to pay the fees for these activities. Somehow, she found a way to make it happen, even while struggling to make ends meet.

I was six years old when I started Little League football. My name was put on a list of first-division players. I can still remember the feeling of excitement I got when I got the call from the football coach, letting me know that I was now a member of the Cowboys football team. The fact that he chose my name off a list, without seeing me play, did not make me any less excited.

I was smiling as I went over to the rec department to get my helmet and shoulder pads. As for my pants, side pads, hip pads, butt pad, knee pads and cleats, my mother had to buy those at Ludie's, the local sporting goods store.

Then it was time for tryouts. The coach needed to see what skills I had and what position I could play. We had boys on the team who could play one or two positions, but the coach saw something special in me. He realized I could play multiple positions.

I could run fast, catch, and tackle. I had a level of hand-to-eye coordination unusual for someone of my age. And I was slippery and hard to tackle. (As I mentioned earlier, I had learned this from Dexter while watching him play.)

It's true what they say about us Black Americans having strong bones and broad shoulders and being faster and quicker than most other human beings. We seem to have been created to be faster and stronger than others.

As a race, we've endured so much, both physically and emotionally. Trials and tribulations—including slavery!—have made us superhuman in terms of our physical strength and resilience. We are relentless, resilient overcomers. Like many other Black Americans, I was blessed with unbelievable athletic abilities and gifts.

Any time I was involved in sports, the coaches and the parents of the other kids recognized this in me right away. I was always one of the most gifted players on my team. I felt like King David from the Bible. God sought out David for a special purpose. He had brothers that everyone thought should have been king before him.

God saw something special in David—something He could use for his purpose. In the same way, God put something special inside of me that would allow me to survive and overcome a traumatic, life-changing event at eighteen years old.

God has a calling on my life. It wasn't until after my accident that I would realize the fullness of His purpose for my life. That's when I came to understand that God wants to use me in a special way to reach people. There was a purpose behind the pain I endured from the accident.

Even when I was still very young, I already sensed that God had something special in mind for me. I thought that being an athlete was my special gift. But I seemed to have magical powers and all sorts of special gifts.

At only six years old, I was already a born leader. I was without the guidance or support of a father, and yet I was able to overcome every obstacle. I learned on my own and helped other kids, not only in sports but in school and in their daily lives. I tried to help everyone become their best selves.

In all areas of my life, I noticed people recognizing that I was special. Every time I went anywhere as a kid, whether it was church or the home of a friend, I could see the way people reacted to me. Their expressions told me that they had noticed something special about me.

After the accident, I became more spiritual. As I became closer to God and his word, I felt a burning desire to help people overcome their trials, tribulations, and adversity. This was the adult version of the kind of help I offered as a kid. Now that I had some maturity and spirituality to back me up, I was able to be even more effective.

Five

On the football field, I quickly learned the plays and picked up on everything the coaches were showing and teaching me. After several practices, they gave me the nickname Torpedo because I was cat quick.

Not only was I impressive to the coaches but I had all the other parents talking about me, as well. They all agreed that, "This little kid is special and is going to become something one day!"

Some of the other kids had fathers in the household to teach them how to play football. You would think that not having my dad around would have made things difficult for me, put me at a disadvantage, and put me behind compared to the other kids. I didn't let it.

I knew I had to put in extra work. Every time I watched a football game on T.V., I paid attention and learned by watching. I also learned by watching Dexter, my cousins, and other good players as they played football.

Our team didn't have a great season that year. In fact, we won only one game. After the season was over, though, I heard what everyone was saying about me—how I was especially gifted and quick. It got me very excited. All during that first season, I had been hoping that my mom would be able to afford to pay for me to play again.

Now that I had my first season out of the way, I would rush home to do my homework. After my homework was done, I would grab the football and go outside to sit with my grandfather.

After Big Daddy had his legs amputated, his favorite thing to do was sit outside in the sun. He would make his way down the back steps of the house—which wasn't easy wearing his wooden legs. Then he would settle into his favorite chair and share his wisdom with me. He did that every day unless it was raining.

"Lee Mar," he would say, "a lot of other kids your age have both parents in the house. But you, your brother, and sisters, you're all at a disadvantage in life. So, you have to work extra hard!"

(As I mentioned earlier, even though my name was Gabriel, I always used my middle name, Lamar, while I was growing up. But Big Daddy always called me Lee Mar, as if my middle name was made up of two different names.)

When Big Daddy told me that I needed to work harder and strive harder if I wanted to be my best, I believed him and took it to heart. That was my grandfather. He didn't pamper us or make us think life was going to be easy. From day one, he set the standard of going out and getting what you wanted out of life. At the same time, he let us kids know that he believed we had it in us to succeed.

I'm sure the wisdom he imparted to me gave me the confidence I have today. I know that I may not be the best person or the most educated. I also know that God can use anybody—and He is using me to reach people who don't think they can move forward from tragedy, adversity, or trauma.

By the time I had spent a while sitting and talking with Grandpa in the afternoons, everyone else would have gotten home from school. That's when I went next door to the home of my grandmother on my dad's side of the family to meet up with my cousins. We would go out in the street to toss the football around and play touch football. Then it was time for dinner.

Back then, it was hard for Big Mama and my mother to put food on the table. There were times when we had to get eggs from the chickens and vegetables from our garden, just to make dinner. Or, my mom and grandmother would go to the grocery store and pick up the cheapest meats, along with whatever else was on sale. When I say the cheapest, I mean exactly that.

On Saturday mornings, I got up and started watching cartoons. I couldn't wait until the afternoon so I could watch college football on T.V. Then on Sundays, I watched NFL football on T.V. I was only seven at the time, but I wasn't a typical seven-year-old. As I watched the college and pro football players, I saw them executing more advanced versions of the same plays the coach was teaching us.

I was excited to know that the next season was fast approaching. So were the coaches who were wanting me to play on their football teams and hoping that my mom would be able to afford to put me back into football. Then the season was upon us, and our home phone was blowing up and ringing off the hook with calls from coaches.

The coach for the Broncos wanted me on his team. That was the team that chose me. After meeting the coach and some of the players, we had our first practice. Boy, did we have some talent on that team. When we played our first game, we blew them out. After we had gotten a few games under our belt, we decided to look up our record. That's when we discovered that we were undefeated, at 5—0. We seemed to be the team to beat that year.

Me and a guy named Tim Sims played both defense and offense. We became known as the dynamic duo. We were the two little thoroughbreds on the team. We had become a two-man show, even though we were team players. The beauty of it was that everyone played their part. It was a real team effort. Playing as a team was what made us so good.

As the season went on, more and more people started seeing what a good player I was and realizing that I could someday become something special in the game of football. I had started thinking about and dreaming of becoming a professional football player and playing in the NFL.

Our team would go undefeated and advance to the Little League championship game—the Autumn Bowl—and face the Monroe Packers, who were undefeated as well. It wasn't much of a match. We ran all over them, and it was a blowout.

Both Tim and I received MVP awards in that game. He got the most valuable offensive player. I got the most valuable defensive player. Winning those awards was the highest honor we could achieve at that point in life.

Any time our team played first, I would stay afterwards and watch the older players play. I liked learning from them by watching. By sticking around and watching those games after our game, I was able to advance my skills.

Unfortunately, that ended up being my final year playing rec football. My mom couldn't afford to pay the fees anymore. But that didn't stop me from holding onto my dream of one day becoming a professional football player and playing in the NFL. The game had become a part of my life. I lived, breathed, and dreamed football.

I would lay down on the floor of my grandparents' house at night, terrified of the rats and cockroaches, and stare up at the ceiling towards Heaven. I knew that I had a special gift that could one day get my mom and all of us kids out of our living situation. I was hoping, praying and thanking God because I knew that He was the one who had given me my special gift.

Six

When we got home after school, we did our homework. When I was finished, I continued to meet up with my cousins and some neighborhood kids to toss a football around and play touch football. The older kids were the team captains, choosing who they wanted on their teams.

Even though I was the youngest kid, I was always picked before the older kids. The captains knew that I was very good and had mad skills. After the teams were chosen, we went at it.

My brother, Dexter, was a great player himself. He never went easy on me just because I was younger. Neither did my older cousins or any of the older neighborhood kids that played ball with us. Sometimes we even played tackle football. Any time the ball came my way, I would catch it and hang on tight, slipping through the hands of people trying to touch or tackle me. Those games made me even tougher and more physical.

We would play until it was about dark and time for dinner. I was evolving and excelling at the game of football. As the year went by, I continued watching and studying the game.

Meanwhile, Dexter started playing baseball. He would only end up playing for one year. I also had an older cousin who had been playing recreation baseball for as long as I could remember. I liked to go to both of their games and watch them play.

As I watched my brother and cousin play their baseball games, I picked up on the game. After the games were over, I went out onto the field and ran around the bases at lightning speed. Then I started going to practice games with my cousin. I would be out there shagging (catching) fly balls. The team also let me take batting practice with them.

Again, my abilities were evident to both the coaches and parents. They all saw something special in me when it came to the game of baseball. Now, when we all went outside to play after school, we weren't only playing football. We had another game we could play.

We would find a piece of plywood and prop it up against a fence or a tree for a backstop. Then we'd get a tennis ball, and a bat or broomstick, and choose teams. Once we had our teams picked out, we played what we called fastball.

You should have seen us trying to hit that tennis ball with a broomstick. It was really difficult to do, and that made it hilarious for us players and anyone watching. It prepared me for playing baseball later down the road. It even took my football skills to another level by improving my hand-to-eye-coordination.

One day, we kids came home from school and found Mom in a very happy mood. She was super excited. We all looked at her and each other and wondered what was going on. It turned out that all the work my mom had been doing over the previous few years had finally paid off.

"I can now afford to get us our own place," she told us. "And best of all, it's right down the street from here!"

Mom had discovered some new housing-project apartments being built within walking distance from my grandparents' house. In being able to afford to move us in there, my mother had overcome a big hurdle. This was a major deal, a huge step.

When Mom told us the exciting news, we all started jumping up and down in excitement. It felt like Christmas had come early for us. At the same time, I was sad to leave my grandparents' house, which had been home to me.

I couldn't stay sad for long. I was so excited that we were going to have our own place, within walking distance from my grandparents' house. I knew I would still see them and my uncles all the time, and that made me feel good.

Our new home was a three-bedroom apartment, and we had it all to ourselves. With three bedrooms, my mother was able to have her own room, my sisters were able to have their own room, and my brother and I had our own room. We quickly got used to our new home and settled in. It didn't take long for us to meet some of our neighbors and make new friends.

To furnish our new place, Mom went to a nearby flea market every Saturday morning, looking for bargains. When she had the money to buy something outright, she would. When she didn't have enough money for the furniture, the vendors offered her flexible financial arrangements. The vendors knew my mom and she had built a relationship with them, so, they trusted her.

My sisters decorated their room in girly stuff and my brother and I had ours decorated in nothing but football stuff. We had football designs and logos on everything—sheets, bedspreads, lamps—even the rug.

Christmas was right around the corner. We never expected much in the way of gifts at Christmastime. We knew that our mom was just barely making ends meet. That year, our new home was our main present.

On Christmas morning, my siblings and I woke up expecting very little. Boy, were we surprised when we saw a bunch of gifts under the tree for us! We got the new Atari and a few games to go with it, clothes, and a lot of toys. It was, by far, one of the best Christmases ever.

It turned out that Mom had gotten a check from our father. He was behind in his child support payments and sent the check so he could get caught up on the money he owed. There were, of course, plenty of other things my mother could have done with that money other than spend it on a special Christmas for us kids.

That was my mother. She stayed faithful to us kids and sacrificed what she might have needed for herself. She made sure that we woke up to a joyful Christmas morning. Knowing the sacrifices she made that Christmas morning made the holiday even more special.

I always found ways to keep my mind on football, no matter what other distractions and temptations were around. In the housing complex where we lived, there was a little grassy area. It was actually in one of our neighbor's yards. It was extra soft like artificial turf. The grassy area was small, so my brother, my cousins, and our friends would come over and we would play tackle football on our knees. It was tough playing like that, but fun.

Playing football with my brother, cousins, and friends during that period of my life when my mom could no longer afford to pay for me to be in rec football helped me stay focused. I couldn't wait to get into seventh grade so I could play regulation football.

Seven

My supermom had worked hard to get the five of us out of my grandparents' house and into our own place. She had done what she needed to do to take the burden off her parents. Once we were in our own home, Mom had to find a way to provide food and clothing for us kids.

She bought us whatever was on sale. Sometimes she shopped for us at the local thrift store or flea market. She didn't necessarily buy us the latest, hottest name brands but we were still grateful. Naturally, there was one of us kids who cared more than the others about having the latest name-brand clothes, and that person was me.

Don't get me wrong. I was very grateful to our mother for everything she would buy and do for us. I knew how hard she worked to provide for us. At the same time, I wanted what everyone else was wearing. When I would see my friends that had the latest, I wanted to be like them.

I knew that my mom wasn't in a position to buy them for me. She couldn't afford it. I also knew that one day, I would be able to afford to buy the brands that I wanted for myself. In the meantime, I tried to stay grateful for everything Mom *was* able to do for us, accept it, and happily go on about my life.

My mom really struggled raising the four of us kids without our father's help. She was doing a great job, thanks to God's faithfulness to her, and her own fortitude and faithfulness. She also got loving support from Big Daddy, my grandmother, my aunts, and my uncles.

In some ways, raising my sisters was less challenging for my single mother than raising my brother and me. No matter how devoted she was to motherhood and to our well-being, she could only guide us so far down the road of manhood. Beyond that point, Dexter and I needed a man to step in. Only a father figure could provide further teaching for us on how to be men.

My mother did the majority of the work in raising all four of us kids. She was the one who laid the foundation for us. Then, my awesome grandfather stepped in and picked up where she left off. He helped raise up my brother and me to one day become great, respectful men. But he let us be little boys while we were little boys. He wasn't trying to deprive us of the experience of being children.

When it came to discipline, the entire family pitched in. My mother, grandparents, aunts, uncles—as well as some unrelated adults in the neighborhood who knew our family!—kept us on the straight and narrow. If one of us kids did something wrong or outside our good character, someone would step up.

The neighborhood adults would spank us on the butt with their hand over our pants. When we got home, we got another whoopin' from my mom or Big Mama. They would whoop us with a belt or a switch, either on bare butts or over our pants. Some of these were quick spankings and some of them were longer, but I never considered them abuse.

I didn't like the discipline at the time. Looking back, I can see that it kept us out of trouble and made us more mindful of the things we did. We knew that if we did something wrong, we would get a whooping. The lesson was clear and simple: if you do A, B will be the outcome. It gave me good boundaries in life.

They say that it takes a village to raise a child, and that was definitely true in our case. The entire neighborhood was involved. Don't misunderstand me, though. My mother did not allow just anyone to have a hand in disciplining us kids. She only entrusted us to adults she knew to have good character—people who knew our family.

Back in those days, it wasn't like it is now. Many parents nowadays believe that they are the only ones who should be able to discipline their kids or tell them, "Don't do that!" or, "This is what's going to happen if you do that!"

It's a shame because a neighbor or family friend could be the one who keeps your kid out of trouble, out of jail, and out of harm's way—if they are allowed to say something to the kid when they observe them doing something wrong. They could even keep your kid from seriously hurting themselves or someone else.

Thank God, my mom understood the importance of discipline. She didn't want any of us to get into trouble, end up in jail, get seriously hurt, or hurt someone else. My mom is my world! She is an awesome, incredible, amazing woman. That's why I was on the road to setting her free financially before I got shot—and why I still hope to do exactly that someday.

During summer vacations from school, the four of us kids would get up early to go down to the community center. Kids from the surrounding neighborhoods would come as well.

The community center opened their doors to kids as a way of keeping us out of trouble and giving us something to do for the summer. Most everyone who knew about it would go down there—kids from all the different neighborhoods close to mine.

We went there as soon as we got up in the mornings and had breakfast with all the other kids. Thanks to funds from the city, they were also able to feed us lunch and provide activities for us. Sometimes we played board games. At other times, we played sports like softball and basketball. Of course, the sports activities were my favorite.

At first, I didn't have a clue as to how to play basketball. It was totally new to me. So, I watched the other kids and saw what they were doing. I especially loved watching the older guys play. I knew that one day I would be old enough to get out there and play with them.

I was a very fast learner. I would wait for a game I had been watching to be over, and then I'd go onto the court before they started the next game. I practiced dribbling and trying to make baskets, just like I'd seen the other kids doing. Every summer, I did that repeatedly. It didn't take me long to pick up on the game.

By the time I was old enough to join the older kids on the basketball court, they had already become aware of my football skills. When they saw me playing basketball, they told me that they saw great potential in me. It felt so good to hear this from some great players with college prospects—guys who could someday become NBA players. It was very encouraging to a little kid like me. It boosted my ego and gave me even more confidence.

Back then, there weren't as many sports camps. It wasn't like it is now, with all kinds of camps where athletes could go to evolve, enhance, and refine their skills. We had to learn sports on our own or have someone older teach us whatever sport we wanted to learn.

I often think that if I'd had just a fraction of the resources and support young athletes have at their fingertips today, the sky would have been the limit. I would have become an even bigger sports beast than I did.

My limited resources didn't stop me from becoming a great athlete, though. I had listened when Big Daddy taught me that being average was not good enough. And, just like he told me to do, I worked extra hard and went the extra mile. I knew that this was what it was going to take if I wanted to become great and have a shot at being the best.

At the end of every school year while I was in elementary school, they held a field day, with multiple contests for each grade level. It seemed like every year my class would either win or finish at the top. We had such talented students in our class.

I would win just about every contest, which set me on the path to leadership. Seeing how good and talented I was, the class always voted for me to be one of the captains of our class. The captains were in charge of which students were best suited for a particular activity.

The time was coming for me to go to middle school. In the city of Covington, there were two middle schools—Sharp and Cousins. Friends of mine from elementary school would be attending Cousins. I was in the Sharp school zone, so that's where I would be going.

I was really looking forward to middle school. Once I was in 7th grade, I could play regulation football. I was so hungry for the game of football and my appetite got bigger by the year. I was equally excited to go into 7th grade just to be moving on to the next chapter of my life.

Meanwhile, I still had to get through sixth grade. That school year was all about staying focused on my schoolwork. Mom was very strict. She let me know that I had to get all my schoolwork done before I could even think about playing any sports.

Sometimes, though, I did stay after school and watch the seventh-and-eighth-grade students practice and play their games. Then I would rush home and do my homework. I couldn't wait to get it done so I could get outside and work on my football skills.

On other days, I walked down to the playground and played a little basketball with my brother and the older guys. I always found myself hanging out and playing with guys that were much older than me. I knew that by playing with older guys, I would improve the skills I had picked up when I was younger, and learn new things, as well. Everything I learned would make me that much better and a lot tougher.

The older guys saw something in me and allowed me to participate. I appreciated the fact that they did not take it easy on me, and even pushed me to be my best and keep up with them. I truly feel that hanging around older guys helped me become my best.

The more I realized who I wanted to become and was able to take steps to get there, the more I realized how badly I wanted to help take care of my mother. I was aware of the major sacrifices she made for us, and how she was always struggling to make ends meet. Seeing her struggle drove me even harder. It became my motivation to succeed not only at football but in life.

Mom had made sacrifices, and now it was time for me to do the same. In fact, I felt it was time for me to go above and beyond what she had done. At the end of the day, it was about setting my mom free from struggle.

I had been given a gift that every kid my age wanted—pure, raw athletic talent. I had developed a passion for playing football and sports, and it had become very important to me, and I had been given the talent to really excel at it.

As I neared the end of sixth grade, I got super excited, knowing I was soon going to get to play regulation football. I wasn't the only one. The coaches were excited too because they had heard all the talk about this kid who was so good in rec football.

The time had finally come. I was in seventh grade and eligible to play regulation football. I was no longer limited to playing sports with kids from the neighborhood. Now I would be playing on a team representing my school. I knew that from then on, every school team would get me that much closer to the collegiate and professional football level—and freeing my mom.

First, I had to get through tryouts. During tryouts, the coaches saw the same thing in me that the coaches from recreation football had seen—my ability to play multiple positions. They also recognized right away that I was gifted with special athletic abilities. So, I easily made it onto the team.

There were many talented players that tried out for the team. Those of you old-school players will know what I mean when I say that I played multiple positions—wingback, defensive back, wide receiver, and backup quarterback. I also played on special teams. (Special teams include kickoff, kickoff return, punt, and punt return.)

I had a lot on my plate for someone still so young. I had to learn both the offensive and defensive playbooks. I was definitely up for the challenge, and I embraced the task ahead of me. I understood that in order to be the best, I had to be willing to do to more than the average athlete.

Eight

My grandfather once told me, "Never settle for just being average. Always be willing to do and be more."

When I found the book, *The Prayer of Jabez*, I was reminded of Big Daddy's message to me. The book talks about being a gimper—someone who does a little more than what's required or expected, someone who goes above and beyond.

Every football practice was a workout for me. I had to go back and forth to perfect all three phases of the game—offense, defense, and special teams. That was another way of learning to be even more responsible in life at an early age. I had to be focused and I was, because I wanted to be the best at every position I was asked to play.

In order to be the best on the field, I had to be the best in the classroom, as well. I thought of myself as someone who was focused on my schoolwork. The truth was, I tended to talk a lot and disrupt the class. That got me into trouble.

My middle school counselor, Mr. Hampton, knew that I was one of the kids who was being raised by a single mother of four. He understood that I came from a broken home and did not have a father in the household or in my life. So, he took me under his wing and passed his wisdom along to me. He would talk to me about becoming a man, being responsible in life, and taking care of my mother as a man does for his family. He also showed me how to play chess.

He and other teachers that had me in their classes saw something special in me, just as everyone did. They all came to an agreement to put me in the advanced classes. That move changed me, challenged me, and allowed me to become the student athlete and young man I was capable of being.

They knew that by moving me away from some of my good friends, they would help me focus and keep me out of trouble. Part of their reasoning was that I was doing too much socializing during school hours. And some of my friends were bad influences. I knew that Mr. Hampton was pushing me beyond my comfort zone for my betterment. He wanted to see me grow—and I did.

As I stated in the beginning of this book, this is not a perfect story as I am not a perfect man. I still got into some trouble, just like every other kid. Thankfully, that trouble didn't prevent me from staying focused and doing what I was asked to do and supposed to do, on and off the field.

As the seventh-grade football season quickly approached, I was all set to go and super excited to get back on the field. It was finally game time, after all my hard work, many practices, and plenty of sweat. I was one of the few seventh-graders who were starting players.

There would be a pep rally before the game. I experienced my first pep rally as a sixth-grade student *watching* the football team play. All of us students and cheerleaders got excited and pumped about the opening home game. Now it was my turn to experience the feeling of having everyone cheer me on as I played football instead of just watching.

It was the day of our first game. Our team experienced many challenges during the game, and we lost. We had to get back to work if we wanted to be a winning team. We worked hard at practice games, and I always went the extra mile.

Then I went home, did my homework, and went outside to work on my skills and get better at the positions I was asked to play to help the team. I was definitely a team player, a trait that had been instilled in me at an early age. Every day after I finished my homework, that was my routine.

Meanwhile, as the school year continued, Mr. Hampton and the teachers saw the great work I was doing in my classes. They were blown away to see how much I had improved since they had moved me into the advanced classes.

Mr. Hampton continued his chess lessons with me, playing during lunchtime. He knew that the game challenged me and taught me how to become even more focused. Chess also kept me from getting into trouble—mostly, anyway.

I still got into a little bit of trouble, but nothing so extreme that the school would have prevented me from playing sports. Sports were my thing, and I didn't want anything to keep me from playing. So, I tried to stay focused and keep a level head.

Our football season was nearing an end, and our record hadn't improved much. Overall, we had a fairly decent season, but we didn't do that great. We still had to play our rival, Cousins Middle School. We couldn't stand their team because they always won the middle school championship and had an arrogant attitude.

The Cousins Middle School team had some great players who were very, very talented. They were big, strong, and fast. They knew that we had some great players, as well. Somehow, they found out about me being one of those good, fast players. Some of them knew of me from when I played rec football a few years earlier.

The game against Cousins was the final game of the year. On game day, they had it out for us. They were focused on trying to shut me down, along with the other great players on the team. They focused most of their energy on taking me down.

As the game started, our team held our own. We went back and forth, with each team scoring points. They had thought that they were going to come in and blow us out, but it didn't go down that way.

I switched off between playing offense and defense and was equally strong at both. They tried everything to stop me, but nothing they tried worked. I was catching passes, avoiding their attempts to tackle me, and generally making them look silly.

We played a close game but unfortunately, they won. At the end of the game, a few of their players and coaches came over to me and told me that I was very athletic and talented. I was beyond excited and happy to get compliments from the coaches and players on the opposite team. That was the end of football season.

Basketball season was fast approaching. Right before the end of football season, the new head coach, Mr. Hartwell, had seen me playing football. While watching me play, he took note of my athletic talents and abilities.

After the game, he had come up to me and asked if I had ever played basketball before. Then he asked whether I would be interested in playing on the school team once basketball season started.

I said, "Yes, to both questions…the only thing is, my mom can't pick me up after practices. She's too busy working."

"No problem," he said. "I can take you home after practices."

I can still remember riding home with him in his little Nissan truck that had seen better days. I appreciated his kindness to me.

I ended up having Coach Hartwell as my social studies teacher, as well. He was a funny guy with a great sense of humor. He made social studies fun. Just to make us laugh, he would come to practice with his shorts pulled all the way up over his stomach like the Steve Erkel character from the iconic T.V. show, *Family Matters*.

After school, Coach Hartwell hosted an entire week of basketball tryouts. There were some players who weren't that good at football but did pretty well at the basketball tryouts. As the week went along, he had some of his great players run with the first and second team. At first, he had me run with the second and third team. Then, as the days went by, he also had me run with the first team.

When the tryouts were over, Coach Hartwell had to make some decisions as to who had made the team and who he had to cut. Every day after practice, as he was driving me home, he would tell me how I was doing and what I needed to work on. He let me know that he saw in me the potential to become really good.

Just like with football season, I went home every day after school and made sure I got my homework done. Then I went over to my cousins' house. Both of my cousins were good at basketball and football, but one was an exceptionally good basketball player.

Sometimes we played in my cousins' backyard, where they had a basketball hoop, and I worked on my game. Other times, we went down to the playground and played pick-up basketball games. There were some real superstars at the playground—real talented basketball players like the four Avery brothers.

I was determined to be great at whatever I did. My work ethic was through the roof. The older guys I played sports with saw my determination and recognized my athletic abilities, as well. The guys had all come to see me play football, so they already knew about my skills on the football field. They were really impressed that I was also good at basketball, and they were willing to help me become a good basketball player.

When cut day finally came, I found out that I was one of the twelve who had made the basketball team. I was excited to have the chance to do my part for the team, and showcase my God-given talents. As we were preparing for the beginning of the season, Coach Hartwell started me on second and third team.

As the weeks went by, the coach started to have me work in with the first team. He saw that I was picking up on things and getting better and better every week. Those of us who are athletes know that learning, grabbing things quickly, and progressing comes naturally for us. I still had a way to go in learning the game of basketball but I was already pretty good.

When I first joined the team, I was just playing around with basketball. I didn't have the same level of interest in it that I did with football. While learning the game, though, it began to grow on me. I started to really like playing basketball. The first game of the season was fast approaching. We had really come together as a team.

Then it was game day. Just like with football, we had a pep rally before the game. Boy, was it fun! Once the game started, the coach let a few minutes of play unfold. Then he started to pull players off the bench and sub them in for other players. When he chose me, I got my chance to play in my first official regulation basketball game.

My heart was beating fast and I was nervous. But when I got my first rebound and made my first basket, my nervousness went away. The game moved at a very fast pace and before I knew it, it was over. Unfortunately, we lost.

As the season progressed, our team improved, and we won a lot of our games. Just like with the football team, we had that rivalry between our school and Cousins. We still had to play the big game against Cousins. We had already played them once and they won. We faced each other twice during basketball season, and they were very intense, hostile, and physical games.

The basketball season came to an end. There were still several months of the school year left, so I turned my focus to my studies. Mr. Hampton and the rest of the teachers were proud of me, for both my academic and sports performance.

My 7th grade year would soon be over. I promised myself that over the summer, I would continue to polish my skills in both football and basketball. I had worked so hard in both sports, and I didn't want to let my progress slide. This was no time to rest on my laurels.

During summer vacation, I continued to go outside to meet up with friends and play touch or tackle football. Just like always, we played touch football in the streets and tackle in a grassy area in front of one of our neighbor's houses. I still sought out the older guys because I knew that would give me the best chance of accomplishing my mission to become an even greater athlete.

Meanwhile, my grandfather—the man who set the standard for the men in my family—was dealing with serious health issues and starting to go downhill. No one could figure out what was going on with him. That was taking a lot out of both my grandmother and my mother. When we took him to the hospital, we found out that he had suffered a stroke.

Big Daddy was admitted to the hospital so the doctors could keep a close watch on him. Having my grandfather hospitalized was devastating for all of us. It really tore me up to see the man who had helped raise me lying there in a hospital bed, helpless and unable to even carry on a conversation. I was really hurting that summer but I stayed focused.

After my grandfather had been in the hospital for a week, he started to regain some of his functionality. He still couldn't talk but he could open his eyes and use his hands a little bit. So, they released him. We knew that, even though he was back home with us, he still wasn't well.

Nine

Now that Big Daddy was home again, I went back to work. But while I was working, I was thinking about my grandfather. He was strongly on my mind, which made it hard for me to stay focused on work. I would break down and cry. Then I realized I needed to push through my emotions. That was my way of honoring my grandfather and all the sacrifices and hard work he had put in during his life.

With my grandfather at home but still ailing, my grandmother and my mother had to make sacrifices and alternate in taking care of my grandfather. My aunts also came to see their father and help out when they could.

Meanwhile, the summer was coming to an end and my eighth-grade school year was right around the corner. Eighth grade would be my last year of middle school before heading to high school. I wanted it to be a great year for me.

I was excited about getting back out there and competing in football and basketball again. Basketball season wouldn't be starting until wintertime, but football tryouts were right around the corner. Only seventh-and-eighth graders could play on the football or basketball teams. No sixth graders could play on either team.

The eighth graders who had been on the football team the previous year had graduated from middle school and gone on to high school. That left a bunch of positions open. Meanwhile, new seventh graders were also interested in competing for those positions and trying to make the team.

So, we had to have tryouts. One of the several positions I had played the previous year was backup quarterback. That position needed to be filled again. Several players from both grades were competing for the position, including me. The starting quarterback position was still up for grabs, as well. That's the position I most wanted to play.

I knew that even if I won the starting quarterback position, I would still be called upon to fill in and play other positions on defense. I would give my main focus to the quarterback position, as that was the most important one to me at the time. (Later, my focus would shift away from the quarterback position.) I still trained just as hard to keep my skills polished up on the other positions I would be asked to play from to time.

A week or so after tryouts, I got the good news that I had won the starting quarterback position. Now, it was time to get to work both on the field and in the classroom. I was motivated to stay focused on my schoolwork and do well. I knew that if I didn't get my schoolwork done and pass all my classes, I would be benched until I brought my grades back up.

Nothing was going to keep me from playing football—the game I loved so much.

While preparing for the upcoming season, I had to work extra hard and be the leader my teammates were expecting me to be.

Continuing to take on responsibilities sped up my maturity process. Thanks to Big Daddy, I was already mature for my age. During the years we were living in his house, we had spent so much time sitting together in the backyard, having conversations. He had passed along to me some great wisdom and knowledge about life.

In the period after his health went downhill, when I would visit him, he continued to pass along many things that contributed to my development as a man. Everything was now paying off. I was becoming the young man he had taught me to be. God, I love that man for speaking life into me. He had a major impact on my life.

Our first football game as a team was a home game, with a pep rally beforehand. I was all pumped up and ready to go.

On game day, we got off to a bit of a slow start, but we adjusted quickly. I had a really good game. The entire team had a pretty good game overall, and when it was over, we were the winners.

As football season went along, our team got better but we had our challenges. We weren't the only ones. My grandfather was ailing. Towards the end of the season, the coaches saw that there was something bothering me. They pulled me into the office to ask me what was wrong.

"It's my grandfather," I explained. "He had a stroke and he's not well."

They saw that I was hurting and let me know that they understood and would be there for me.

As I faced the biggest game of the season, I had Big Daddy very much on my mind and heart. We were playing against our rival, Cousins Middle School. When I say they were out to get me and take me down, that's a major understatement. They were trash-talking and using dirty tactics when they tackled me.

I didn't allow it to get to me. The only thing their hassling did was make me get even more focused. I had way more important things to worry about, like the fact that the man who had raised me was on his deathbed. I was hurting badly on the inside.

The Cousins team tried everything in their power to hurt me and take me down, just like they had the previous year. And just like the previous year, I held my own and played a great game. They still won, and that was the end of me and middle-school football. By the next year, I'd be playing for the high-school team.

As soon as football season was over, I had to start preparing for basketball tryouts. Basketball season was right around the corner. Thankfully, I made the team.

The basketball coach knew that I had something on my mind and heart. The football coach must have let him know that I was hurting over Big Daddy's failing health. The two coaches were pretty close.

Just like the football coach had done, the basketball coach, Coach Hartwell, pulled me into his office one day after practice. He talked to me about how I was feeling about my grandfather and let me know he would be there for me and help me get through it.

Mr. Hampton remained my counselor all the way through eighth grade. And he also took on a mentorship role with me. He was there for me, making sure that what I was going through didn't negatively affect my schoolwork.

He knew that it very well could have affected my entire school experience, on and off the field. Sometimes, he would call me into his office to play chess. He knew that this would help ease my mind. He was very supportive.

I tried not to let what I was dealing with over Big Daddy's health keep me from being prepared for the start of basketball season. We played several practice games and then it was time for the real thing.

Sadly, midway through the season, my grandfather passed away. I had been dreading that day for so long, and now it had happened. I had lost the man who raised me and my three siblings, the man who I looked up to as a father, the one who spoke life into me. It was Big Daddy who had built the foundation for our family and taught me how to be man.

I was devastated, crushed. My grandfather's death affected all of us but it seemed to have an especially big impact on me. I was really taking it hard. Mr. Hampton was there for me. He helped me through this tragedy and helped me stay focused. Miraculously, I was able to finish out the basketball season.

Our team had a pretty good season, despite the fact that I was mourning the loss of Big Daddy. The ending of my eighth-grade year was also bringing me to the end of my time in middle school. I was excited about attending Newton High and going to the next level, not only in sports but in life.

During the summer between the end of middle school and the beginning of high school, I was grieving—but I was also continuing to work on my skills in both football and basketball. I was determined to keep pushing forward and become the best player I could be. It wasn't easy, given the way I was feeling.

During that same summer before high school, Mom somehow managed to find the money to buy us a house. So, we moved from the apartment in the housing projects off Highway 36 and into a house in Settler's Grove.

As the beginning of my first high school semester drew closer, I found out that I had to take a physical in order to be eligible to play sports. Unfortunately, there was a fee to take the physical. My mother could not afford to pay the fee for both my brother and me.

The school ended up offering the physicals free of charge. I'm not sure what Mom would have done if that hadn't happened. Maybe she would have paid for just my brother, since he was older. Luckily, we never had to find out.

On the Saturday morning the free physicals were being offered at the school, I woke up very excited. I knew that both the varsity head coaching staff and the coaching staff were going to be there. They had all seen me play football when I was in middle school, so they were familiar with me.

When I got there, I saw coaches from other sports, as well. Once I was checked out and passed my physical, the coaches talked to me and were excited about having me play for them.

My brother and a few other upper classmen who lived in our new neighborhood would once again be playing on the varsity football team, just as they had the previous year. The team was holding a summer workout-and-conditioning training camp to prepare us for the fall football season.

This camp was not a sleepaway camp. It was held at the high school. This training camp was right up my alley and being offered at no charge. I took advantage of this opportunity to work on my skills and get better. It also gave me a jumpstart over other freshman who were too busy enjoying their summer vacation to be thinking about football.

I would catch a ride to training camp with Corey Anderson, a senior who lived about three houses up the street from us. The workouts consisted of weightlifting, conditioning, and spending time on the practice field.

Only certain positions would be on the field at any one time. Since I could play multiple positions, I chose to play the cornerback as my main position. It was a highly skilled position, and I had to be quick and fast. I was both. I was asked to work out with the receivers, quarterbacks, and defensive backs. We had a very talented group.

One cornerback by the name of Dale Carter would go on to become a first-team All American and a four-time Pro Bowler. Dale was the best in his position on our team.

He was a beast. He became a mentor to me. I would watch him and mimic his style of play. Of course, I added my own little twist, but believe me, there wasn't much that I needed to add.

Head Coach Morrow, the defensive coordinator coach, Harold Johnson, and the defensive back coach, Coach Mansfield, all saw my talent and athleticism. They were just as impressed as everyone who had watched me play when I was younger.

After we had been working out for several days, Coach Johnson saw Corey and me leaving to head home. He stopped us and said to Corey, "I'm so glad Tuggle's been able to catch a ride with you every day! There's something special about this one."

Oh, was I excited and pumped to be hearing this from the head guy for the defense!

There were a few changes made on the coaching staff. The new defensive line coach, Coach Autry, had the whole defense pumped. One day at the summer workout practice, the entire defense had to hit and push the sled. I was right in the mix with those upper classmen, handling my business, hitting and pushing that sled.

That was the day that Coach Autry said, "Look at this rookie. Look at how impressive he is. Y'all going to let him show you up like that?" From then on, the team called me Rookie.

Just as they did every summer, the varsity football team went to Villa Rica, Georgia for sleepaway camp at West Georgia College. Since a linebacker named Phillip Benton and I had been working out with the varsity team at the school training camp, we were asked to go. I couldn't recall any freshmen being asked to go before, so it was a real honor for us.

I went home and started telling my mom and friends about it. Some people were excited for me, and some weren't. They thought I was being arrogant because I was excited. The truth was, I was as humble as they came, and didn't bother anyone. But being humble didn't mean that I had forgotten about all the hard work that led to me receiving that invitation.

There was a whole lot of jealousy going on. The jealous ones did not understand that it wasn't *luck* behind me getting to go to Villa Rica. I had *earned* my invitation. I had worked hard to improve my skills during times when my friends were out enjoying their vacations.

My work ethic was through the roof because that's what I was taught by my mother and grandfather. They had instilled in me at an early age the importance of working hard for anything that you wanted. They also made sure I understood the reality that nothing is given to you in life. You have to go out and earn it.

People would come up and try to pick fights with me because they were jealous that I got to go to Villa Rica and they didn't. This jealousy followed me from my childhood Little League teams all the way into my life in high school. It was a real shame.

Ten

The day I was to leave for football camp at West Georgia College was fast approaching. There were some things that my brother and I had to have for camp—toiletries and bedding. So, my mom, being the supermom that she was, made another sacrifice to make sure we had the things that we needed.

One Sunday morning, we departed for West Georgia. The offensive team was on one bus and the defensive team was on another. We had been told that this camp was known as a rough, tough camp. It wasn't for wimps, mama's boys, or crybabies. For starters, the weather was likely to be brutal. They were forecasting high humidity and temperatures close to 100 degrees.

Before we left, the coaches were razzing us, saying, "Okay, guys, take one last good look at your parents. You're going to be wishing you were back with your mamas when we're your daddies for the week!"

We boarded the buses and took off. The camp was sixty to ninety minutes away. It was a fun road trip. We had a chance to get to know our fellow teammates better and bond a little bit. Once we arrived at the camp, we were assigned our roommates and given the schedule breakdown for the week.

We were housed in dorm rooms furnished with two cots. My assigned roommate was an upper classman who played defense.

In the mornings around 6:00, the coaches came around, banging on doors and yelling that it was time to get up and get ready for our 8:00 a.m. practice.

We would be fed breakfast, lunch, and dinner at the camp. We had three practices games daily and a scrimmage game on Wednesdays. The parents were invited to come up for a visit on Wednesdays and watch the scrimmage game.

Any time a rookie goes to camp with the big boys, he's going to be tested. I was no exception. The first night, some seniors came into my room while my roommate and I were both asleep, flipped my bed over until I fell onto the floor, and then ran out. I had been trying to get a good night's sleep so I'd be ready for the first day. I got flipped out of bed instead.

Thankfully, I eventually fell back asleep. When I woke up the next day, I went back and forth between being angry and laughing. I said to myself, *Whoever did this to me is about to find out they messed with the wrong rookie. It's on!*

After we got dressed, we all headed to the cafeteria for breakfast, I acted like I didn't know anything about what had happened the night before. But I had an idea of who the pranksters were because I had heard them laughing and recognized their voices. I was just biding my time.

After breakfast, we headed to the field for our first day of practice. That's when I found out why the camp had a reputation for being hot. I couldn't believe how hot it was so early in the morning.

We broke up into groups by positions. They allowed people who wanted to play multiple positions plenty of time to learn those positions, as well. I had four positions I wanted to learn—defensive back (DB), wide receiver, special teams, and quarterback. I was a busy guy. Since I played multiple positions, I started with DB, my primary position.

Camp was tough, just like everyone said it would be, but I was up for the challenge. I was a warrior and one of the most competitive players on the team. Our DB drills were very physical. We worked on our hip work and footwork, as well as tip ball, breaking on the ball, pursuit, back peddling, angle tackling, and face-up tackling. And, boy, were we doing some hitting and running of the ball.

Having great hip work, footwork, and instincts were key to becoming a great DB. I had all of that going for me already but I wanted to perfect my skills. After the first couple of days at the camp, the coaches let me know that they were impressed with my performance.

The point of the camp was to get away from everything and everyone, better yourself, and come together as a family. That team spirit reminded me of the movie, *Remember the Titans*. If you dropped out, you were letting the team down, not just yourself. It was all about team building.

Not all the players at camp were pumped about being there. Camp had just started and some of the players were already over it. Coaches had caught players on the phone, asking their parents to come get them because camp was too hard and too hot. What a bad move on their part, and, boy did they pay for it.

These players had made a commitment by coming to camp, and they broke it. Quitting was not an option. Once you were in, you were in. If you backed out, you paid a penalty. Quitters wouldn't be let back on the team. The coaches who were coaching the team for the fall didn't want any quitters on their team.

Meanwhile, those pranksters were still trying to break me in as a rookie. One day during our lunch break, they snuck into my room and soaked my bed with water. I had to hang my sheets out the window of the room. Thankfully, I found the wet sheets during the daytime. So, the sheets and the mattress both had time to dry before bedtime.

Just like I did the first time they pranked me, I said to myself, *They're about to find out they messed with the wrong rookie!*

While the guys I thought had soaked my bed were in another player's room playing cards, I snuck into their rooms and went into their bathrooms. I opened their toothpaste and put it in their cleats.

At the break during afternoon practice, we were all standing around the water station. Suddenly, their shoes started foaming and their feet started to burn. They didn't know whether to laugh or get mad, and they did a little of both. Everyone on the team was laughing and cracking up. My revenge prank didn't stop them from messing with me, though. After practices, they continued to pull pranks.

Wednesday was great. That was the day when the parents came to the camp to watch us practice. The players were happy to have their parents there and spend some time with them. As you know, my brother and I only had one parent in our lives—our mom. Unfortunately, she was working hard to provide for the four of us kids and she couldn't get the time off work.

While most of the other players were spending time with their parents, I spent that time on the field, working hard to get better. And while I was on the field, the pranksters were still doing their thing. Went I got back to my room, I found all my clothes that had been in the dresser drawers thrown around the room.

While the pranksters were running out of my room, they ran right into our Defensive Coordinator, Coach Johnson. He stopped them in their tracks and asked them whose room they had been in, and why they were running out of there so fast. Then he looked into the room and saw all my clothes scattered everywhere and the room in a total mess.

The coaches had heard that there was some pranking going on, but no one really knew who was involved until they got caught. Or, I should say, until *we* got caught.

After seeing my room in a mess, Coach Johnson took the pranksters to his room to have a talk with them. They confessed and told him that it was my room they had ransacked. Then they ratted me out for my revenge prank. What had started out as us all having fun had turned into us all getting into trouble.

Now, Coach Johnson sent for me. When I got to his room, I confessed to what I had done and explained that

I'd done it to get back at the pranksters. I admitted that I had been just as wrong and that I knew better. But, like I told Coach Johnson, they had messed with the wrong rookie.

I may be a little bit on the quiet side, but I'll get back at you if you mess with me. I know we're not supposed to repay evil with evil—but I didn't want to seem like a chump. If I'd let it slide, I would have been sending the message that I was soft and anyone could walk all over me.

It turned out that the guys who had been messing with me were five seniors—Coach Johnson's top defensive players from the previous year. The coach was deeply disappointed in his leaders. He was also disappointed in this freshman. He and the other coaches had been looking at me as one of the young and upcoming leaders.

After our evening practice and dinner were over, everyone else went off to enjoy their evening, but Coach Johnson had the six of us pranksters out on the field. He had us running sprints and hills, doing backwards-and-forwards bear crawls, barrel rolls, wheelbarrow tuck-and-rolls, and pushups. He pushed us until we were dead tired and it got dark outside. He made sure that we paid for what we'd done and wished we hadn't done it.

When we got back to our rooms, our teammates were teasing us and laughing at us. We were totally wiped out and didn't have the energy to care about what they were saying or doing. All we wanted was to take a shower and get into our beds. I sure did have a good night's sleep. I slept like a baby. Lord knows, I had earned it.

In the morning, I got mad respect from the upper classmen because I had fought back when the pranksters started messing with me. I didn't allow anyone to roll over me and get away with it. They loved the fact that I was a fighter.

The team had been having a great camp overall. And, other than getting into that little bit of trouble, I had personally been having a good football camp so far. After such a good night of sleep, Thursday would end up being my best day at camp. I had a great day because I had perfected the DB drills by then.

I was on my way to becoming a great DB, receiver, and special teams player, and making a name for myself. At the same time, I was becoming better at the quarterback position. All the coaches let me know they were very impressed with me and saw something special in me, just like they had when I was younger.

We got up the following morning, a Friday, had breakfast, and had a good productive morning practice. Then we headed back to our rooms to shower. Now, it was time to pack our suitcases, load the buses, and grab some lunch before heading back to Covington.

As we left, I said to myself, *Man, what a tough, brutal week it was, but I survived it. And I feel like I'm a better athlete now.* When we got back to Newton High, boy, were we glad to be back home.

The beginning of school and open house for the freshmen was only a few weeks away. Before we even started school, we had a Friday exhibition game. We were playing against Fayetteville High on their turf.

Open house came and I went to get my schedule, see where my classes were, and meet some of my teachers.

They all seemed nice. I was really looking forward to the start of school. The following week was the exhibition game at Fayetteville High. We had a great game and beat them like they had stolen something.

The week before school started, my mom had to take us kids shopping for school supplies and clothes. She did her best with the money she had to spend, but it wasn't easy because there were four of us. So, she couldn't buy us a whole lot.

Finally, the first day of high school was here. I was so excited to be starting high school and getting reunited with some of my old elementary school friends. Some of them had attended Cousins Junior High so I hadn't seen them in years, other than when we played the Cousins' football team.

We had a week to prepare for the first varsity football game—a home game. The week before the game was brutal, just like football camp. We were going at it extra hard.

Between preparing for the game and adjusting to my new classes, I had my hands full. I had taken on varsity as well as JV because I wanted the extra opportunity to polish my skills. It was huge for me to be a freshman on the varsity team. Some of the other freshman football players were jealous of me because I got to play on both the varsity and JV teams.

I didn't find their jealousy surprising. I used it as greater motivation to become as great as I could be. Freeing Mom financially was still my main motivation for pushing so hard. I was determined to pursue my dreams and try to make it into the professional football league.

One day when I was a professional football player, my mom wouldn't have to work.

My first week of high school was behind me, and now it was game week. We had a great week of focused practices, going at each other hard. Of course, I couldn't just focus on the game. I was still getting adjusted to my new school and I had to stay focused on my classes, as well. So, I went at it hard, both on and off the field.

All the coaches were excited about the season. They felt we had a very talented team and could do something great. The Thursday before the game, we were allowed to wear our team helmets and shorts and do a walkthrough to get familiar with the game plan. Then after practice, they passed out jerseys for us to wear. I was given a jersey with the number eighteen on it.

Then it was finally Friday evening and time for the first (varsity) game. Being that this was the first game of the season and it was being held at home, we had a pep rally beforehand. This was a much bigger rally than the ones we used to have in middle school. The gym was really rocking.

They introduced all the seniors and then the entire team, with me and the only other freshman being introduced last. After the pep rally, we had the pre-game meal in the lunchroom. They fed us a full meal and then for dessert, they served us a lot of fruit. That was a healthy way to load up on the carbs we needed for energy for the game.

After we ate, we headed down to the locker room. They started passing out our football pants. Then, anyone who had areas of the body that needed taping for extra support used that time to take care of it. The rest of us used that time to get our minds right for the game. Then it was time to head to the stadium, which had been rebuilt during the off season.

It was exciting to be the first team playing in the new stadium. There was only one problem. Both my brother (who played running back on the same team I was on) and I had told our mother that we needed new cleats. Since she had to work that day, she couldn't get to the store until she got off work.

When it was pregame warmup time, my brother and I were stuck. Mom still hadn't shown up with our cleats. So, we had to play the pregame in our old shoes. Thankfully, by the time the game started, Mom had shown up to the field. Just in the nick of time, my brother and I were able to trash our old cleats and quickly get into our new ones.

Eleven

It was game time. We came out of the locker room pumped up from our coach's speech and the team chaplain's prayer. The beating of the drums from the band pumped us up even more.

As we ran out onto the field, busting through the banner, the crowd went crazy. They were finally seeing the team that had the potential to bring a state championship to Newton County. I had the chills and butterflies in my stomach, being on the field in the new stadium.

We lost the coin toss and were on offense first. We drove down and scored on the opening drive. Now it was time for the defense to get on the field. Boy, did we have some talent, between the new players and the returning players on defense.

Because I'd had such a great summer camp, the D.B. coach was torn about who was going to start in the cornerback position opposite Dale Carter. The coach told me to stay in his hip pocket in case he needed to put me in.

After a couple of possessions on defense, the coach called on me to go out on the next possession. I was getting ready to play in my very first varsity football game, early in the game, and I was only a freshman.

The other team had a huge running back and they ran a running play to my side. Everyone was holding their breath, thinking that I was going to get run over. What a surprise I gave everyone when I came up on that big running back and tackled him.

As the game went on, I made some great plays, breaking up some passes that were thrown my way. That's when I truly got mad props and respect. We went on to win the game big, and that set the tone for the season.

After the game, everyone headed over to McDonald's, the usual hangout spot. A lot of upper classmen, as well as some great football players who had already graduated, came up and give me props for my performance as a young player.

They told me, "You're going to be something special! You're super talented." Hearing that boosted my confidence even more.

My weekends were filled with football, as well. On Saturdays, I went about my usual routine of watching college football. My favorite teams were the Georgia Bulldogs and Notre Dame.

I watched pro football on Sundays, no matter who was playing, but I especially loved to watch the Atlanta Falcons play. Whether I was watching college or pro football, I became a real student of the game. I was determined to gain as much knowledge and understanding of it as possible.

I mostly focused on and studied the position I played—cornerback. I really paid attention whenever cornerback Deion Sanders was playing a televised game.

It was easy to see that he was destined for a great career. I also studied the players who were in the other positions I was asked to play from time to time.

Monday after school let out, we were back at practice again. It was the first week of junior varsity (JV) football. All JV games were held on Thursdays, and varsity games on Fridays. I was one of the starting cornerbacks on the JV team. We had a good week of practice for both varsity and JV.

Our first JV game was a home game. Thursday came and I was ready. In addition to playing cornerback, I played special teams on JV kickoff, kickoff return, punt, and punt return. I also played backup quarterback and receiver.

I had a lot to remember, but I was a gifted athlete with God-given raw talent. I was up for the challenge and ready to do whatever it took to help the team.

As the game got underway, we really had our hands full with the other team. We were losing at halftime. Some of the varsity coaches and players came over after their practice and gave us a pep talk. That seemed to do the trick because after that, we started playing like the football team we were capable of being.

We went on to win the JV game. The entire team did well, and I also had a great game personally. The varsity DB coach and the defensive-coordinator coach watched our game and were both very impressed with my performance.

When we got back to school, we were given the jerseys we would wear during Friday's varsity game. This time it was an away game, so we would be playing on the other team's home turf. When game time came, the DB coach was torn. He didn't know whether he wanted to have me or the senior start the game.

Just as he had done in the first game, the coach put in the senior but told me to stay in his hip pocket in case he needed me. The game was tight all the way through, and the coach didn't feel like he needed to put me in very much. So, I only got to play a few downs on defense. We ended up losing the game but because it was so close, we all held our heads high as we walked off the field.

Monday, we had practice for both the JV game on Thursday and Friday's varsity game. At practice after the drills and before the scrimmages, the defensive coordinator told the entire defense, "There are no starters for the upcoming varsity game. There's so much talent on this team, I'm comfortable starting any one of y'all! So, you're going to challenge each other for a starting position."

I challenged the senior cornerback. I beat him out and won the starting position for Friday's varsity game. I was so excited, knowing I would be the starter for the game. The game was going to be a regional varsity game, which carried greater importance in terms of our overall standing in the conference.

After we were finished with the challenges, the coaches called the first offensive starters onto the field. The JV defense went out onto the field to run the opponent's defensive plays that the first offense would be facing in the actual game. (The JV defensive players were always present at varsity games, in the event one of the varsity players got injured and needed back-up step in.)

The first defensive starters were on the opposite end of the field, going over some of the other opponent's offensive plays. The coaches watched film of our opponents' past games to try to determine what plays they might use in any given game.

The head coach called for me to be on JV defense to run the opponent's plays, having no idea that I had won the starting position for the varsity game. I was usually one of the starters on JV defense.

I wanted to become great at the position, so I would play both JV and varsity just to get that extra work in. I practiced all week with the first defense until Thursday and then I would go play with the JV.

Thursday, I played the JV game and had a good game. Friday came and I was pumped to be a starter for the first time in a varsity football game. To be in this position as a freshman was unheard of, considering the amount of talent on our team.

As I said, this was going to be an away game. We got to the stadium and went through our normal drills. At last, it was game time. Since we won the coin toss, we had the choice of receiving or being on defense. We chose to be on defense first, which meant we would be on offense in the second half of the game.

On their very first play, they ran the ball to my side. I came up and laid such a hard hit on that running back, I knocked him completely out of the playing field. The entire defense came up to me, jumping up and down.

Right before halftime, the quarterback made a pass to the receiver who was coming inside. I read the route the receiver was running and picked off the ball, for my first high school career interception. Not only that, but I returned the ball fifty-five yards for a touchdown!

We went on to win big. From that moment on, I was being talked about at Newton High as an up-and-coming star. I was having such a great season.

Being one of the young studs on the team, all the young ladies saw me as a big-time football star and wanted to be with me. I was already popular with the girls but boy, did this take things to another level.

I was being asked out by freshmen girls, sophomores, juniors, and seniors, and loving every minute of it. There were plenty of people who also resented me now, but I didn't let it derail me. I stayed humble and focused.

On the academic side of my school life, it was progress report time. The school didn't play when it came to our schoolwork and classes, and neither did the coaches. Anyone who got a grade of C or lower had to run hills. If you had an F and were failing, the coaches would run you until you were dead tired.

I got A's and B's—but I also got one C. I had to run hills, but not too many. No one wanted to run hills. Any time I had to, I used it as motivation to stay focused, not only on the football field but in my classes.

I kept getting better, right along with the rest of my team. Week after week, we were playing lights-out football and beating top teams like Clark Central. We even beat the Cedar Shoals team. They were every bit as good as we were and had a bunch of talented players on their team.

We made the top ten in the state and made a run for the playoffs. Newton had not been in the playoffs for some time. Brookwood—a team that was in our region—was number six in the state. We traveled to them and beat them on their turf. That resulted in us winning a spot in the playoffs.

Our first playoff game was the first one held in Homer Sharp Stadium in years. We won. Next was a rematch against Brookwood from the game three weeks earlier, with us hosting the game. Boy, were they hungry for us, but we were just as hungry. We beat them in a close game, just like we did the first time.

Now, we moved onto the state quarter-final round. We would be traveling to Memorial Stadium on Friday and playing Southwest DeKalb. We spent a week preparing for the game. Game night was forecast to be one of the coldest nights of the year. They were planning a big pep rally for us—one that turned out to be the best I had ever experienced, by far.

On Friday, we loaded up the buses and took off to Memorial Stadium. We had an escort from the Georgia State Patrol, which made us feel like we were big time. After arriving, we unloaded the buses, went into the locker room, and got into our uniforms. Then we headed onto the field for our pregame warmup.

This was the game everyone was waiting to see—our number-one defense against Southwest DeKalb's number-one offense. What a showdown it was going to be!

Even though it was freezing outside, the stadium was packed on both sides. The game got underway, and we started battling it out. Both our team and theirs were performing well. I personally made some great plays. In the last quarter, the game came down to the wire.

We played a great game but ultimately lost to them. It was the end of a great football season. We had thought for sure we would make it to the state championships, and so did everyone else. It didn't work out that way, but we were proud to have made it as far as we did.

Throughout the football season, the freshmen basketball coach had been in my ear, asking me to come play for him. By the time football season finally ended and I had the energy and focus to consider his invitation, basketball practices had already started.

After barely a week of rest, I was back at it again, this time with basketball. I was able to skip tryouts because the coach already knew that he wanted me on the team—but I was a little bit behind everyone else. Thankfully, it didn't take long at all for me to get up to speed.

This would end up being the only freshmen team I played for as a freshman. I played backup to the guard position and got several rebounds in the game. I played a few basketball games and then it was time for our varsity and JV football banquet.

As everyone was arriving, we were all standing around joking and talking about our season and the Southwest DeKalb game. It was great to see everyone. They were all commenting on how I'd come in, started as a freshman, fit right in, and had a great season so far. They were also talking about how I'd gone from football to basketball, with only a week of rest in between, and how fast I'd caught up to everyone else.

Dinner was served and it was a good one at that. Shortly after dinner, they started passing out letter jackets for those who didn't have one. They also passed out region champ patches. I was so excited to be getting my letter jacket.

Then they started passing out trophies to those who'd had a great season. Not only did I get a letter jacket but surprisingly, I was awarded the JV defensive MVP player of the year trophy! To take that home as a freshman was a major accomplishment. I added it to all of the other MVP awards I had earned when I was playing Little League football.

I'd had a pretty good basketball season and it was getting close to wrapping up. Meanwhile, both the track-and-field and baseball coaches were asking me to come out and play for them.

The funny thing was, I had never played on a baseball team in my life. I had only played unofficial games with my brother and some of our friends in the neighborhood. Yet, the new baseball coach saw something in me, just like the coaches in the other sports. He saw that I had speed, a strong arm, and could catch. He knew he could teach me the rest once he started training me.

The rest of the kids played only one sport, so they had some free time. Not me. I was determined to get bigger, better, faster, and stronger, and become an all-around great athlete. So, I figured, *Why not participate in the other sports?*

I wanted to master them all. I knew that doing so would enhance and evolve my athleticism and at the same time provide me with more options when it came time to play pro ball. That way, I wouldn't have to rely on just one sport.

I was asked to try out for the JV baseball team. Surprisingly, I made the team. They saw the potential for me to become a great baseball player. Track and baseball would be going on at the same time, so I was going to have to split my time between the two.

While on the track team, I worked on my form and speed, running the 4-by-400-meter relay and the 440-yard dash. The track coach tried to get me to run the hurdles, as well, but I didn't have time to do all that and also go to baseball practice.

In baseball, they showed me how to hit properly and catch a flyball. And because I was fast, I was taught how to steal bases. They positioned me mostly in center field but from time to time, I also played left field. Everyone was amazed by how quickly I picked up the sport and how fast I progressed.

Twelve

Both my baseball and track seasons were underway. I was working hard and staying focused on my responsibilities and my mission in life. Track season ended before baseball. I'd had a very good season.

The baseball coach asked me to join the varsity team to finish out the season. What an honor! I was brought onto the varsity team to be an extra outfielder and base runner. Throughout the season, I evolved and excelled and took my baseball skills to the next level. There was no doubt that I was a gifted kid who could play any sport and be good at it.

I never wanted to limit myself when I knew I had been given so much talent. My grandfather once told me that I should never sell myself short. So, I left everything on the field every time I went out there, regardless of what sport I was playing.

As the season and the school year came to an end, we missed the playoffs, but I wasn't too disappointed. What a freshman year I'd had, playing several of the most popular sports. I had great momentum going into my sophomore year.

I was ready to spend the summer working at becoming the best athlete—truly great. I had already started receiving football recruitment letters from colleges who wanted me to come play for them.

When I was younger, mom found a way to buy school clothes for us kids, even though she couldn't really afford to. I always picked out expensive ones.

"You need a job, Lamar, so you can buy your own clothes! I can't buy you these expensive clothes."

Well, the time had finally come that I was old enough to get a job. That was so exciting. When I got my summer job, working construction, I looked at it as my second job. My first job was to work on perfecting my sports skills.

It would have been hard for any kid my age to work a physical job all day, come home, and put in the hours to perfect my sports skills. But I was dedicated and determined, and always up for the challenge.

I never forgot my grandfather's words. "Life isn't going to be easy," he told me, "especially coming from a single parent home. You will always be at a disadvantage compared to the kids who come from two-parent homes. You will have to do more and work extra hard to make things happen."

So, that's what I did after work. I would go and participate in the football summer workout program being held at the high school and overseen by the football coaches. My summer was very full.

A few weeks before the start of my sophomore semester, it was time to go to West Georgia for football camp again. When I showed the coaches what I could do in each of the positions I played, they were very impressed. They could see that I had been putting in some hard work over the summer.

By the end of the summer, I had earned enough money to be able to buy most of my own school clothes. By the time I purchased a few pieces of clothing I really liked, I had spent almost all the money I had earned. Mom had to pitch in financially and help me buy the rest.

Paying for my clothes out of my own pocket was a big reality check. It really helped me understand why my mom hadn't wanted to buy expensive clothes for me.

Seeing me try to buy expensive school clothes with my own money made my mom laugh. "See?" she said. "I told you. You want me to spend my money on those clothes, but it's a different story when it's *your* money."

I was excited to get my class schedule and start my sophomore year of high school. We had two weeks to prepare before the start of football season. Once the football season started, I would end up getting even more football letters from colleges.

Thanks to all the hard work I had put in, I was named one of the starting cornerbacks. I was going to be on all the special teams, as well. I would also be playing position of receiver and third-string quarterback whenever I was needed. It was quite a workload, but I was the perfect candidate to take it on, and totally up for the challenge.

Our team wasn't as strong as we had been the previous season but we were pretty good. During the first game of the season, we had a tough go of things right out of gate. Not only that, but I realized right away that the schedule for the football year and my workload were going to be tough on me. I was playing too many positions.

After playing and losing the first game, I was already tired from playing both offense and defense, as well as special teams. After all the work I had put in over the summer, I thought I was in shape. I had quickly found out that I was wrong. I put in more work to get into shape, after practices and at home after getting my schoolwork done.

By the time the third game rolled around, I was in better shape. I had gotten used to playing both offense and defense and being on special teams. So, I was less tired after the game. I had put in the extra work and gone the extra mile, and it had paid off.

We were halfway through the season with a five-hundred record. I was having an outstanding season, adding some more interceptions and touchdowns to my resume. College football letters started coming in even more from top Division 1 schools.

It was time for progress reports at school. Just like the previous school year, those students with C's, D's, or F's had to run hills. And, just like the year before, I got one C and had to run hills. The school kept it consistent across all sports. They wanted to make sure that all of us athletes were performing academically, as well as in our sports.

In the second half of the season, we still had to face most of our region opponents and compete for a spot in the playoffs. Unfortunately, after a hard-fought season, we came up short and missed the playoffs.

Just like the previous year, before football season had ended, I had the JV basketball coach in my ear, talking to me about playing on the team. Also like the previous year, I was accepted onto the team without going through tryouts, which had already taken place. The players on the team were mostly the same guys from our freshman team, with a few additions.

I was preparing for the upcoming basketball season, but I wasn't that into it. My mind was on football and on playing baseball. Even though basketball wasn't my top priority, I still worked my butt off in the position of number-two backup guard. We didn't have the best basketball season and it couldn't end fast enough for me. I was excited to get into baseball.

I was playing on the varsity baseball team, which was exciting. There were high hopes for this year's team. I decided that I would take a break from running on the track team so I could give my entire focus to baseball. The track coach was very disappointed. Even though I wasn't on the track team that season, I still made time to work on my speed.

I was determined to become one of the best at whichever position I played. So, I was working out and training hard for the upcoming baseball season. I was quickly becoming one of the coach's favorites, thanks to my awesome work ethic.

He was impressed with my arm strength and wanted to see me pitch. So, during practice, he had me take my place on the pitcher's mound and pitch to the catcher. It went well. So, now he knew that I was capable of being a relief pitcher if we ever needed one. Our team had high hopes for a great season. We were excited over the possibilities.

We were on fire as we kicked off the season, winning the first eight out of ten games. Heads started turning and teams were hearing about the Newton Rams. (The ram was our high school mascot, so all three sports teams—football, baseball, and basketball—had the Rams name.)

I wasn't a starter at the beginning of the season—but I was the main base stealer. I also went in and closed out a few games in the outfield. Then, toward the end of the season, I started some games as well. The competition came down to the wire, and we won our region, moving into the playoffs for the first time in decades.

We kept the momentum going, winning the region and moving into the semifinals. We were a couple of games away from going to state championships. Unfortunately, we fell one game short. I didn't let that demoralize me. Instead, I vowed to work even harder during the summertime and off season.

Another school year was coming to an end, and what a great year I'd had in sports. I was happy about that—but it wasn't enough for me. As far as I was concerned, I still had work to do. I was determined to not only become great but be the best.

That summer, my mother got me a summer job at her place of employment. I worked there in the mornings. When I got off work, I went to my "second job"—getting even better at the games of football and baseball.

By that time, I had decided that those were the two sports where I wanted to put my focus. Letters were flooding in from colleges who wanted me to play on their football teams, and I was getting letters here and there with baseball offers too. The letters were coming in so fast and piling up so high, I had to find a designated spot to keep them.

I didn't have a normal summer like other kids because I was so focused on working toward my dream of becoming a professional athlete and setting my mother free. I had bigger plans and a greater vision than just having fun over the summer.

By now, you've figured out that I wasn't an average kid. There was something special about me that no one could figure out. I had really excelled in my sports and had become a beast when it came to working out.

This was the first summer we weren't able to go to West Georgia for camp. There was no money in the budget for the football program to send the entire team to a sleepaway camp. The coaches found a quarterback/receiver camp down at Furman University in South Carolina instead. There were just enough funds in the budget to send two of us players.

I was already going to be the starting cornerback once the season started—but I was also going to be the backup quarterback and one of the primary receivers. So, they chose to send me and the starting quarterback—a guy named Jay—to the camp. (I wouldn't be perfecting my cornerback skills at this particular camp.)

We took off on a Sunday morning and headed to South Carolina for a week. On the way down, Jay and I had fun talking about our upcoming season. We talked about baseball as well as football because he was also an important player on the baseball team.

When we arrived at the camp, we started meeting and interacting with some of the top high school players.

Because I was a top athlete in my little hometown, some of the guys had heard about me. Apparently, my reputation preceded me.

I was excited about camp starting the following day, and ready to go. I would be splitting my time between the two positions, just like I had been doing.

As soon as they saw me play, the coaches and other players were saying, "Wow! This kid is really good!"

Thirteen

On Wednesday, they surprised us bigtime when Green Bay's star wide receiver, Sterling Sharp, showed up. He spoke to us and passed along some good advice. One thing he said really stuck with me: "Remember, making it to the NFL isn't guaranteed!"

He ended up sticking around for a while, and later pulled me aside. "Listen," he said, "I want you to know that I believe you have what it takes to make it."

Hearing those affirming words from such a great player was a major boost to my confidence. As camp came to an end, I finished strong.

On the way back home, the starting quarterback and I talked about what a great camp it had been and how much fun we'd had. We went over everything we'd learned and discussed ways to take those lessons onto the playing field and apply them.

This camp really elevated my game. Since I played all three positions, it gave me a deeper understanding of the mindset and thought processes of a quarterback, receiver, and CB—not only *what* they are thinking but *how* they think. Camp took my knowledge of the game beyond that of any average high-school quarterback, receiver, or CB.

My first two seasons had been great but as you know by now, I was always aiming high and trying to be the best. That meant I had to continue to perform and take my game to a higher level. College letters continued to pour in with offers for both football and baseball. This was further confirmation that I had a real chance of becoming a professional football player and freeing my mom.

As my junior year of high school started, I was still trying to add to my school wardrobe when I had the money. It felt good to help lessen my mom's financial load a little bit. I looked forward to the day when I was a professional athlete and could do something big for her—like buy her a house and a car.

I was now a junior in high school. I was all set and ready to go. I was coming off another great summer where I had put in the work to improve my football and baseball skills. I was excited to get back out on the field.

This year, I would be the starting cornerback, the number-two receiver, and the backup quarterback, as well as playing on all special teams. The ultimate goal from the start had always been to play as many positions as possible, be great at all of them, and become one of the best.

As I strived to reach that goal, there were plenty of challenges I had to overcome. Going into the new season, the coaches and my teammates had high expectations of me as one of the leaders on the team. I was determined not to let them down.

With this being my third football season, I had gotten my routine down to a tee. I knew how to stay on top of my classwork while also getting it done on the field. I was having an awesome year with both.

Being a hard-hitting cornerback known for shutting down any receiver who came my way, teams were afraid to throw to my side. And when I was playing in the receiver position on offense, they couldn't keep me from catching passes and scoring. I was now playing at a higher level and really peaking.

We were having an up-and-down season, but I was still performing as the leader they expected me to be. As far as I was concerned, no matter how our season was going, I needed to do my part and give my best to help our team. Unfortunately, it wouldn't be enough.

We missed the playoffs again—but that didn't change the fact that I was already a great athlete. Playing all three positions of cornerback, backup quarterback, and receiver evolved my game to where I became one of the top athletes in the state. I was highly sought after by college football (and baseball) recruiters.

After football season ended, I could have taken a break, but I didn't. I went straight into working on my baseball skills, along with the other baseball players, preparing for the start of the season. There's no question that I remained consistent when it came to working out and improving my skills more and more.

The coaches loved this about me. They recognized that I was a gifted athlete who was not going to content myself with relying on my raw talent. I knew that there was always going to be someone else out there who was just as good or better. I knew that I had to keep putting in the extra work and going the extra mile, just as my grandfather had taught me to do.

I was just as excited about this season as I had been about the previous one. We had lost some great players from the team since then, but we still had some great players ready to step up and replace the missing players.

One day at practice, I was messing around and the coach noticed that I had some smooth hands on the infield. When a ball came my way, I was able to pick it up and throw it to first base in one movement. We were in need of a backup third basemen, so the coach decided to try me out in the backup position. So, now I was a starting outfielder, backup third baseman, and relief pitcher.

As the season got underway, teams that had heard about me through football now had a chance to see me doing my thing in baseball. I played multiple positions in both sports. Once again, everyone was saying, "Wow, this kid is really special!"

They would see me start in the outfield, playing my primary position of outfielder. Then, they watched me come into the infield and take my place at third base. If I had been on another team that didn't already have one, I think I could have been the starting third-base man.

Wrapping up the season, our team won our region for the second year in a row and moved into the playoffs. I was racking up stolen bases and was close to breaking the record for stolen bases in a single season. We missed making the quarter finals by one game, but we held our heads high. Our team had a great season and so did I.

I was determined to make that summer leading up to my senior year the best ever. I was focused, committed, and ready to put in the work. I trained, worked out, and prepared for the upcoming football season. As if all that wasn't enough, the baseball coach put us in a summer league.

That summer, a few neighborhood guys and I got a hip-hop dance group together. We called ourselves Amerikka's Most Wanted. We practiced, got really good, and competed in talent shows and other events on Fridays and Saturdays.

I'm sure you're wondering how I had time to practice dance when I had football practice and baseball summer league going on. Well, somehow, I found a way to stay involved with dance without it interfering with either football or baseball. I stayed focused because my dream, my goal, and my vision of setting my mom free was so important to me.

The starting quarterback on the football team had just graduated. I knew that, as the backup from the previous year, I would be expected to throw my hat into the ring for the position.

I had worked so hard to become one of the top cornerbacks, and that was my focus now, not becoming starting quarterback. With me just starting my senior year, I was striving to be the next Primetime Deion Sanders. I knew that the better I was in my senior year of high school, the better my chances would be to play college football for a Division 1 school—and hopefully make it to the NFL someday.

It didn't much matter whether I *wanted* to be the starting quarterback or not. I knew that I was the best player for the job, and I was willing to do whatever was best for the team. So, as the summer came to an end and school started, I went to tryouts and tried out for the quarterback position.

I was chosen as starting quarterback. In addition, I was still expected to fill in as backup for the other positions, just as I had done previously. I didn't want to juggle being starting quarterback, backup, and CB. But, what could I do? I didn't feel like I could refuse the position.

As if all that wasn't enough, our head coach had left at the end of the previous school year. Thankfully, installing a new head coach was an easy transition. They gave the job to our defense coordinator. I was just glad they didn't bring in someone new.

Every time I put on any sports uniform, I had the goal of freeing my mother in my mind. So, with every sport and every position I played, I strived to be great. My mom was my constant motivation.

Football recruitment letters kept pouring in, and it looked like I was going to have a choice as to where to play college ball. My mother told me, "I want you to be close to home. You know how I feel about flying!"

Georgia Tech was nearby and high on my list. They were consistently trying to recruit me. They invited me to come tour the campus for both football and baseball. Even though Mom was in support of me attending Georgia Tech, she was unable to go with me for the school visit. So, my brother-in-law came along.

Gabriel Tuggle

When I got there, they extended an invitation for me to attend every home football game they had during their upcoming season. (At the time of my campus tour, it was coming up on football season.) They rolled out the red carpet for me and the other players they were recruiting. Since they had won the national championship the year before, every game was hyped and filled with excitement.

With me in the quarterback position, football season did not get off on the best footing for either the team or me personally. I did a pretty good job as quarterback, but I was making mistakes that caused us to lose some close games. Our defensive team was getting slaughtered in their passing game.

Our coaches made the decision to switch to the backup quarterback. That decision was welcomed by me. It allowed me to go back to my bread-and-butter role—being the hard-hitting, shut-'em-down cornerback/receiver, and handling my duties on special teams.

I continued making plays on both offense and defense, increasing my interceptions, and scoring touchdowns. It was my best season by far. Unfortunately, we ended the season with a record that was only a little above average and missed the playoffs again. We had hoped that we'd have a better season, with twenty-two returning seniors and a talented team.

Meanwhile, I had completed almost all the classes in my major that were required before I could graduate. The school allowed us to work in order to make up missing hours from afternoon classes, as long as we attended our morning classes. So, during the second quarter of my senior year, I signed up to get into the work study program. I got a job doing shift work at KFC.

The work-study program at our school was set up on a quarterly basis. There was no minimum number of quarters we had to stay in the program. We could do work-study for as many or as few quarters as we liked.

Here's how it worked: School hours were from 8:00 a.m. to 4:00. I would go from 8:00 to noon—lunchtime. If I wanted to stay in school all day, I could take electives in the afternoon until 4:00. Or, I could have a job in the afternoons and that would count as school hours.

I only worked three or four afternoon shifts each week. That turned out to be a win-win situation for me. That left me with three or four afternoons each week to train hard for the upcoming baseball season. And I had some money in my pocket from working.

I trained with Timmy Hyers. He had been drafted by the Toronto Blue Jays the previous year, right out of high school. He lived locally and had been on my baseball team. He was a pure, natural hitter who was consistent with making contact with the ball.

Timmy always got a base hit at the very least. He had a real sweet swing as a leftie. It was a rarity to have a leftie with as smooth a swing as Timmy's. He led the team in all stats, except for stolen bases. That record belonged to me.

On the days when I wasn't working, we would meet up to work on my hitting and pitching. He also hit fly balls to me and ground balls on the infield. I was putting in the work so I could become a beast in baseball that season, just as I had been in football. The work ethic instilled in me from an early age was through the roof, and I was determined to be the best and succeed.

During my senior year, I continued to be highly sought after by top Division-1 NCAA colleges in both football and baseball. I had narrowed it down to a couple of schools. I was planning to make my final decision around the beginning of baseball season.

I was on the cusp of accepting an offer to play college ball. That would have put me four years away from the start of setting my mom free.

Fourteen

On February 10th, 1991, I walked up to Spanky's house and went inside. I could hear everyone hanging out in the back room, so I headed in there. All the guys were joking around and I joined in the fun. I was happy being with the guys and having a good time.

I said something teasing to Spanky in that same spirit of fun. It was meant to be funny.

When they heard the funny thing I'd said, everyone in the room busted out laughing—except the guy I had said it to. In that very moment, Spanky happened to be cleaning his Smith & Wesson .44—one of the most powerful handguns in the world.

I could see a bunch of bullets on the bed. I assumed that he had emptied them all out of the gun before he cleaned it.

"What'd you say, motherfu****?" He pointed the gun directly at me.

His response to my teasing remark would be the last words I heard before becoming the miracle I am today.

I woke up in a strange place and discovered that I had monitors with wires and tubes attached to me. I had no idea what had happened to me.

Dr. Gropper came in and informed me that I had been shot in the head. "With the damage being so severe," he said, "it's a miracle that you survived! You must be superhuman!"

He explained that the bullet he removed from my head had entered on the side of my brain where my speech center was located. Other brain functions were affected as well. As the doctor was talking to me, he had to lean in close and speak into my ear because I was too weak to do anything but lay there, helpless.

Before I was discharged from the hospital, the doctor gave my mom the prescriptions she needed to get filled for me.

"It's important that you take all the prescriptions," said the nurse, "but it's really imperative that you're consistent in taking the one for the seizures."

My grandmother had an account with the pharmacy on the square in the little city of Covington. That's where I got all my prescriptions filled.

When I arrived home, I found that my room had been all tidied up and prepared for my recuperation. It looked very inviting. My medications had already been filled and were waiting for me on my nightstand.

I had such a great, awesome support system in my family. They saw what a difficult challenge and a long uphill battle I was facing on my road to recovery. They all pulled together and helped out in any and every way they could.

A home healthcare nurse came to the house three days a week for the first couple of weeks. This made things a little easier for my mom and my family. The nurse led me through speech therapy and physical therapy. We worked in my room, and she also took me outside for walks.

Two weeks of in-home care was all that our insurance would cover. After that, I went three times a week to physical therapy and speech therapy at a facility recommended by my doctor. The doctor felt that I was strong enough by then to go to outside physical therapy.

Before she left, the in-home nurse had taught my family how to work with me. On the days that I didn't have outside therapy, my family worked with me at home on my therapies. Everyone in the family pitched in and helped.

In physical therapy, my faith continued to be tested. I was faced with so many challenges, there were days when my frustration built to the point where I burst into tears. I would think about how everything I'd been working toward had been within reach, at last. I had been so close to freeing my mom financially with the money I would have made playing pro football.

If that had happened, I would have been able to ease my mother's financial burden. I wouldn't have had to keep pushing so hard. Now, I was right back in the position of having to crush it every day, just to be able to recover my health and reach a point where I could function like I had been able to before the accident.

I felt like giving up—but there was something inside of me that overpowered that spirit. It was a still, small voice, telling me, *You can do this! Just be patient…and trust me!* I listened to that inner voice and trusted it. As it encouraged me, I started to get stronger each day.

Before the accident, I had scheduled a time to take the SAT test. Now the time had come. I wasn't thinking straight at the time. I said to myself, *Well, I paid for it…I guess I'll show up.* And that's what I did—I showed up.

Unfortunately, that was about all I was able to do. As I slowly walked into the classroom, I saw the expressions on the faces of the teacher and the few other students who were already sitting there. They were truly shocked to see me. This teacher hadn't been my teacher but she taught at my school. She had heard about my accident through the grapevine, along with all the other students in school.

"What a shame that you had to show up today in this condition. They should have refunded your money or rescheduled your test for another time."

The fee I had paid for the test was nonrefundable, so I had shown up. I was trying to be responsible, going through the motions. I remember sitting in that classroom in a daze. I didn't feel all the way inside my body. And, I was still struggling to hold my head up because my neck was still so weak.

One afternoon, I came home after physical therapy and a follow-up with the doctor and decided that the time had come. I needed to face one of my fears and do something I had not done since my accident.

I walked out the door and up the street. I was heading to the house where I had gotten shot. I was going to visit Spanky, the guy who had shot me.

It seems kind of backwards, doesn't it? He never came to see *me*—the guy whose life he almost ended!—while I was in the hospital recovering from the life-threatening injury he had caused. No one from his family came to see me in the hospital, either. And none of them had come to see me since I had gotten home from the hospital. Yet, there I was going to visit him!

When I got to Spanky's family's house, I knocked on the door. His older brother answered. When he saw me, he looked shocked. He just stood there, like he had seen a ghost. All he could say was, "I'll go get him." Then he turned around and went and got Spanky.

Spanky let me into the house without meeting my eye. He couldn't even look at my face. It was very uncomfortable for us both. What an awkward moment!

I didn't have my full speaking capacity back yet. I was still unable to speak full sentences. All I could manage to say was, "Why?"

He dropped his head, refusing to look at me or speak to me. He did seem sorry and remorseful. In fact, he seemed to be eaten up inside by what he had done to me. The sad part was, he didn't take that opportunity to apologize.

Why am I surprised? I asked myself. *He didn't even have the decency to come see me in the hospital during the entire time I was there!*

I kept thinking about the fact that Spanky hadn't apologized or come to visit me in the hospital. *Does he think my life has so little value, he doesn't need to apologize after nearly killing me?* I asked myself.

I got so upset, I had to leave. By the time I got back home, I had tears running down my face. I went into my room and sat down on my bed, continuing to cry. I couldn't stop thinking about how Spanky had ruined—and nearly ended!—my life and failed to apologize for doing so.

My mom walked into my room, grabbed me, and said, "Everything is going to be alright, Lamar. I'm just glad you didn't die on me when the doctors wrote you off. I'm so happy you're here. We're in this together and we're going to get through this together. It's just you, me, and God. He's the only one who can and will get us through this!"

My mother has always been my rock. She said, "God spared your life, son, and I'm so thankful and grateful."

Hearing my mom say these things to me, something came over me. I felt a major internal shift. I started thinking about how badly I wanted to be the best. I wanted to be great. I thought about how hard I had trained for football and baseball. I thought about everything else I had worked so hard for in my life.

Now the stakes were even higher. I needed to fight for *my life*. This was way more important than anything else. I started pushing myself even harder. I became determined to not only recover but become better and stronger than ever. As I pushed myself harder, my faith strengthened right along with my body.

No matter how strong I got in body and spirit, there were times when I was grief-stricken over all I had lost. It was so hard to accept that I was no longer the old Lamar. I was no longer energetic or able to move around easily. It was hard for me to walk straight. I fumbled my sentences when I tried to speak. I would be in my room and bust out crying.

My mother and grandmother were such strong believers in God, the greatest one of all. They were the ones speaking faith and life into me. They kept encouraging me daily because they knew how badly I needed it.

My friends told me that Spanky was torn up about what he had done. He carried that burden. It's such a shame that he passed up the opportunity to unburden his heart. I've forgiven him and I wish him only the best. I've dealt with the trauma and hurt related to him and the accident by praying and asking for strength.

I also dealt with the trauma by crying it out. I sat in my room, reading through get-well cards and looking at photos from football and baseball. I'd had a promising career in football ahead of me, a promising future. With one bullet, Spanky stole that from me.

I thought about all that had been taken from me, and I let myself experience grief over the loss. I felt the hurt over what Spanky had done to me and let the tears flow. In this way, I healed, little by little.

I distanced myself from him for a while. Not being around him helped me to heal. We saw each other from time to time because we lived in the same neighborhood—but it was rare. I would be on the front porch and see him up the street, playing. I thought about how he had taken away my promising career. I felt a combination of sadness, hurt, disappointment, and anger.

I hurt for years after the accident. I cried and asked, "Why me?"

It has been thirty years since my accident, as of February 10th, 2021. What makes me different from other trauma patients? I have overcome a major traumatic event and have recovered most of my functionality, all thanks to God. It's so miraculous.

When it was time for my next follow-up with the doctor, I got good news. He was amazed by how well I was doing. He could see that I was getting better and stronger all the time.

He said, "I'm going to go ahead and release you to return to school…but only half days for now."

As I said earlier, I hadn't been going to school full-time before the accident either. I would go to school in the mornings and work at KFC in the afternoons.

"…That way," the doctor continued, "you can keep your afternoons free for physical therapy."

During the time that I was hospitalized, Dr. Gropper had told me that I would never be able to play football again. In this doctor's visit, he reiterated it.

"I want to make sure you understand, Lamar, that your football career is over for good. You won't ever be able to play football again."

"No matter how much I heal or how strong I get?"

"No, I'm sorry. A hit to the head at this point could be lethal, after everything you've already been through."

I burst into tears and started crying. "But what about all the hard work I put in, going the extra mile to become great?"

My mother was with me at the appointment. I turned to her and said, "Now, my chance to free you is gone, Mama!"

"Son, that's all fine and good. But having you here is way more important."

At the time of my February accident, I'd had one quarter of my schooling left to complete before I could graduate from high school. On the day I returned to school, the coaches, teachers, and students were all shocked to see me.

Everyone was amazed by the fact that I had survived such a terrible accident. Most people would have died from the shooting. So, no one at school thought I would make it or that they would ever see me walk into school again.

The school administrators allowed me to break the no-hats rule. Because I had scars on my head from my surgery, I was allowed to wear a hat to cover my scars. Before the accident, people at school were loving toward me. When I returned to school, the amount of love I was receiving (and returning) was unreal. My homeboys were especially glad that I was back.

I continued to go to physical and speech therapy each afternoon after school let out. Everything was getting easier. I was becoming stronger and faster. My speech was improving. But I was still heartsick over losing my sports life.

Sometimes I went and sat in the bleachers and watched the baseball team practice. It was tough being able to look but not participate. Watching them, I reflected on all the hard work I had put in, and knew it was all going to waste. I was crushed.

It made the baseball players happy to see me in the stands, and that kept my spirits up—but the entire experience made me very emotional. It was especially tough watching them play home games, and not being able to perform in front of people who knew and loved me.

Fifteen

Let me tell you a story about my awesome, amazing, incredible God. One day while the baseball team was practicing, the coach saw that I was getting better and stronger. When I felt like I was up to it, I would walk down to the field and participate a little bit in the practices, informally.

The coach ordered me a baseball cap helmet for protection in case a ball accidentally hit me in the head. He allowed me to start tossing the ball and playing catch with the team. Gradually, I was able to work my way up to fully participating in the practices.

At first, it felt a little awkward to be throwing a ball. It was my first time picking up a ball of any type since getting shot. On my first few throws, the ball went off in wild directions. Eventually, my body remembered how to throw and my throws straightened out.

Each day, the coach had me do something a little bit different. One day, he would have me out there catching fly balls and grounds balls. He even had me doing light overhand pitches from the pitcher's mound, which was a surprise to everyone.

The players, parents, and a reporter for the local newspaper who used to cover our games were amazed. They wondered how I could possibly be out there doing what I was doing, so soon after my life-threatening accident.

Even though they were watching me with their own eyes, they could hardly believe what they were seeing. It must have seemed like they were watching a cartoon or movie superhero. The speed at which I was progressing was incredible. Each day, I grew stronger and got back a little more speed, but I still had a way to go.

At first, the coach didn't allow me to accompany the team to away games. Then that changed, and I was going with the team to their away games. I wasn't a participating member of the team during games—only during practices. But I sat in the dugout, supported them, and cheered them on. In that way, the coach allowed me to be part of the games. He knew I had been one of their top players.

Even coaches and players from other teams were glad to see me, and so were reporters. Everyone had heard that I'd been shot in the head at point-blank range and nearly died. They too were amazed to see how well I was performing.

This was crazy considering that a few months earlier, I had been in the hospital, and the doctors had pretty much given up on me and written me off. Now, here I was, back on the baseball field, about to crack the starting lineup. I already knew that I had an amazing work ethic and the way I trained was off the charts, but this was unheard of.

The coach saw that I was getting stronger, so he made me a backup outfielder. During one game where we were winning, the coach put me in to pinch hit. I shocked everyone, including myself, when I ripped a line drive right up the middle. People in the stands, as well as players on the other bench, stood up and started clapping and cheering.

Our bench started jumping up and down, chanting, "He's back! He's back!" I stood on first base, crying tears of joy.

Our last home game was on senior day. A newspaper reporter sat with me on the end of the bench and interviewed me so he could write an article about me. The article turned out to be great, and really special. It was entitled, "A Gun, A Bullet, A New Beginning."

This reporter could tell that I was no ordinary human being. He could see that there was something special about me—something no one could really understand. I was amazed by it, but I didn't understand it myself. It is not for any of us to understand.

Baseball season was over and now it was graduation time. With graduation approaching, I started to get very emotional. My emotions were all over the map.

I would say to myself, *Wow, here I am about to graduate from high school! How does that sound when I nearly died a few months ago and my life was pretty much over? It looks like God had other plans for me.*

Yes, all the offers to play college football were gone. And, so was my dream of ever playing in the NFL. The odds of making it to the NFL were slim, but I knew that I would have been one of those who made it. Now I knew that God had a plan for me that was even greater than playing in the NFL or major-league baseball.

But then I would get to thinking about the terrible, tragic accident that changed my life, and break down crying. I was obviously still dealing with a lot of trauma from the shooting.

I couldn't wrap my mind around why such a tragedy had happened to me. I kept going over all the different possible scenarios that could have gone down that night. I asked myself, *What if I hadn't gone up the street that night to Spanky's house? What if I had just gone home?*

I thought about all my friends who had gotten scholarships. They were going to college, playing football and other sports, and furthering their education. I should've been right there in the mix, going to Georgia Tech or a top NCAA Division 1 school.

I tried to tell myself, *Well, it must not have been in the cards for me.*

Graduation was finally happening. We had a big graduating class and more scholarships than any class prior to ours. We graduates were seated in chairs in the middle of the gymnasium, and our loved ones were sitting up in the bleachers surrounding us.

An announcement was made: "Will everyone who has a sports scholarship please stand!"

I dropped my head and started crying. A classmate sitting next to me grabbed me and hugged me and said, "Everything's going to be alright, Lamar."

I wanted to believe that but it was easier said than done.

Right before they started calling names and giving out the diplomas, they said, "Lamar Tuggle, would you please stand?"

I stood up, totally surprised. The school recognized me for what I had gone through and how I had come back from an accident more tragic than anyone in my small town of Covington had ever endured or even heard about. They talked about how resilient I was and how determined I was in my recovery.

I looked out at the audience, trying to find my number-one fan—my mom. There she was, crying. She couldn't believe it. Her baby, who just a few months earlier had been written off by the doctors, was now graduating and being recognized by the school. My grandmother was there, as well, along with one or two of my siblings.

Since my last name started with a T, I knew it would be a while before my name was called to accept my diploma. While I sat there, waiting, I wondered what was next for me. *What am I going to do? I couldn't handle college right now...*

There was only one thing I *could* handle right then—focusing on getting back to 100%. At the same time, I knew that it wasn't in my personality or my character to just do nothing.

Before I knew it, they were calling out the last names starting with T and it was time for me to accept my diploma. As I got up and started walking across the stage, all my classmates and just about everyone in the audience stood up and started applauding. Once again, I saw my mom burst into tears.

My mom wasn't the only one. Many of my classmates and their parents knew they were watching a miracle walk across the stage. They were moved and amazed. I was overwhelmed by it all and got very emotional. What an awesome, amazing feeling to know that I was graduating despite what had happened to me, and that I had the support of everyone around me.

After the ceremony, the first person I wanted to see was my mom. I ran up to her and as soon as we started hugging, my tears started to flow. Then people started coming up and asking me questions like these:

"How are you doing now? How are you still here? I heard that the doctors had written you off!" And, "How did you survive a forty-four-caliber shot to the head? That should have taken your head off! I can't even imagine what that must have been like."

"I have one three-letter answer for you," I said, "and that answer is God!"

Everyone was telling me that I was lucky to be alive and they were right—sort of. But it wasn't luck. As I said, it was God!

I also had many people coming up to me and telling me how sorry they were about what had happened. They all said, "You had it all right in the palm of your hands! You were one talented dude!"

"Thanks," I said, "but please, don't be sorry. I'm still right here!"

I thought I had used up all my tears and couldn't cry anymore—but then tears of joy started rolling down my face. I wasn't the only one, either. Plenty of my classmates were right there with me, in tears.

There was a graduation party being held that night, and most of my friends were planning on going. They were insisting that I come along, so I did. Well, you know how wild graduation parties can get, and this one was no exception. There was drinking, partying, and having fun. In fact, some of it was a little too wild for me. I was still in recovery.

Everyone was celebrating and excitedly talking about college. It was mind bothering to hear everyone's conversations about college, but I was happy for them at the same time. After a while, my classmates stopped the festivities and honored me again. And once again, I got very emotional.

We had a strong, tight circle of friends, and the special bond of love we shared between us was unbreakable. No one could come between us. Standing there among my close friends, my thoughts returned to the question of what was next for me.

Tomorrow has to come, I said to myself, *and then what?*

It was late by the time the party wrapped and I got home to bed. I was exhausted but I couldn't fall asleep. I just lay there, staring up at the ceiling. I found myself asking *Why me, God? Why me? What's next for me in my life?* I burst into tears.

My brother, Dexter, heard me crying and woke up. "What's wrong, little brother?"

I couldn't speak.

He grabbed me and hugged me. "I know," he said. "I know."

I was leaning on his shoulder, crying, saying, "Why, why, why me? I never in a million years thought something like this could happen to me!"

We sat up and talked a little while. "I was four years away from setting Mom free from all her hard labor, pain, and suffering, Dex! She made so many sacrifices for us, more than we can even count…and they were going to be over soon. I was going to be able to really free her. I can't stop thinking about that. It keeps playing over and over in my head. Now it's never going to happen."

Knowing that there was nothing I could do to change what had happened, I had only one choice: to stay focused on getting back to 100% functionality and move on with my life.

Once I had accepted that I had no choice but to do everything in my power to recover and move forward, I tried to make my peace with the accident.

I had made up my mind before the accident that I would be going to a top Division 1 college and pursuing my dream of becoming an NFL player. Or, if that didn't pan out, I would become a major-league baseball player. Either way, I had been planning to play pro ball and set my mother free. That was my goal.

For some reason, God has bigger plans for me—plans beyond my own ideas and imagination. I know that there's something special I am meant to do with my life. Even knowing that, I am stuck with some big questions.

I ask myself, *How did I get myself here? How will I bounce back from this? What did I learn from this tragic, life-threatening accident?*

It nearly cost me my life, and it did cost me plenty!

Sixteen

Just like many of us in the black community, I was raised up from an early age with my grandparents and my mom. They instilled in all of us in the household the love of God and the love of church. These things are still so important to black families today.

I wasn't completely living my life the way I should have been at the time of the accident—but I wasn't a bad kid. I didn't get into a lot of trouble. I did my share of dirt, but I knew right from wrong.

As I've said throughout this book, I always knew that I was created to be—and do!—something special. I knew deep down that I was different, that I wasn't the average kid. I also know that many people throughout my life before the accident saw something special in me. They always say that other people can see in us things we can't even see in ourselves.

I started thinking even more deeply about these things as I tried to get myself and my life back to 100%. I've recovered about ninety percent, but I'm still determined to get to 100%.

There are decisions we make that put us in bad places and bad situations and cause us to lose everything—even our lives! The decisions we make affect not only ourselves but our family, friends, and teammates.

It's easy for someone to say, "You shouldn't have gone up to that house on the day of the shooting!"

I nearly lost my life because I decided to go up to that house on the night of the accident instead of going home to get ready for school. Oh, how that decision affected my family, friends, teammates, and a whole lot of other people, as well.

We have to start making better decisions and smarter choices in life. We have to think about the consequences, repercussions, pain, and trouble that our decisions might create. We have to consider the cost of our decisions.

We must do our best to make good decisions but we also need to understand and accept that there are things in life—tragic, hurtful, bad things!—that are unavoidable. They are part of our journey. I think of Jesus during His time on earth. He ran into troubles and adversity on His way to fulfilling his purpose. So, what would exclude me from having my own share of adversity along the way?

As I look at Spanky's history, I'm not surprised that he shot me. He was known for fighting and carrying a gun. He used to carry it when we went dancing at nightclubs and talent shows. He was someone who was prone to overreact to things and to want to retaliate.

That should have been my sign to get out of the group right then and there. I had so much going for me and so much to lose. I should have changed my surroundings—but, like many of us, I was just having fun outside of football and baseball.

Well, speaking from experience, I feel that I can encourage you to run the other way if you see any signs that someone you're hanging around with has a history of being a troublemaker. Change your surroundings or your friends, especially if there's a gun involved! There is so much at stake.

Because of the decision I made that led to my tragic accident—an accident that nearly cost me my life!—I'm terrified of guns. Whenever I hear someone say that they have a gun, or hear anything involving a shooting, I take off running like Forrest Gump. Speaking of Forrest Gump, remember the part when the old lady was sitting on the bench with Forrest, and he was holding a box in his hands?

The woman asked, "What's in the box?"

Forrest replied, "My momma always said, 'Like is like a box of chocolates. You never know what you're gonna get.'"

That quote makes a lot of sense to me. Life is just like that! You never know what you're going to get.

I had so much going for me. I had the future in the palms of my hands. I had my goals in sight. I was very close to setting my mom free. I never expected to get shot in the head point-blank with a .44 caliber gun. It was totally unexpected and caught me and everyone else in the room off guard.

So, to all of you who think you're untouchable and have it all together, especially you talented top athletes who think you have everything going for you and nothing could happen to you, I'm sorry to burst your bubble. God knows, I don't want anything bad to happen to you. But I am a man who knows that no matter how great you are, devastating things can happen.

I ask you to please humble yourself. Remember that no one is invincible. Consider your decisions carefully.

Sometimes we need a reset and a fresh start. I truly believe that this is what God is doing in my life. I feel like He is saying to me, "I'm trying to get you to see that there's another direction, a better path I'm trying to take you down. Just like I redirected that bullet so it didn't kill you, I'm trying to redirect your path."

I know that while I go through this process, I have to shift my mindset and redirect my thoughts. I need to start thinking differently. Just know that things can—and will!—be redirected in your life, as well.

Your situation may be different than mine but know this: God has the right to interrupt your dreams and your plans as He did mine. Just know that your life doesn't have to stop or end just because He decided to interrupt your dreams and plans.

Please, don't let it upset you or weaken your faith. Just embrace it and know that He has a better plan for you. You just have to seek Him and get into His presence.

When the surgeon came out of the operating room and told my mom that he did not expect me to recover enough to live a normal life, he seemed to have given up on me. He seemed to have written me off. But God stepped in and said, "No, I'm not done with him yet. I have work for him to do."

The fact that I've recovered as well as I have—well enough to be writing this to you now!—should tell you that your situation isn't hopeless. God can step into any situation, and turn it around for His good and yours, just like He blew breath back into my life and set me on a new journey.

I have had to make some major adjustments in my life since my accident—but I know and believe that God has a different plan for me. Everything happens for a reason. With this new journey that God has me on, I'm here to tell you that God is real.

Sometimes in life, we get to the point where we feel ignored, wonder why terrible things happen to us, start questioning God, or wonder if maybe we just don't matter to God. You're reading the words of a man who has experienced the power and the mighty hands of God. Now that He has given me a second chance at life, I'm learning to trust, to lean on, and believe in Him even more.

I could have given up on life, but God (and my grandfather) instilled in me the determination never to give up or quit. Don't be a quitter. Keep fighting. That's what I'm going to do, and I hope you do the same thing. Never give up, even when your situation seems hopeless.

I may not be able to see what God has in store for me but that's where my faith comes in. I have to just believe and trust that there is something greater for me. My faith—and yours!—is going to be tested continually. I'm sure you've heard this a million times, but here is number one million and one: *Faith is the substance of things hoped for, the evidence of things not seen.* (Hebrews 11:1.)

When all the odds were stacked against me and I was in the darkest time of my life, I overcame it by His grace and mercy. And by His grace and mercy, I'm still here. God had His hands on me the whole time.

The odds may be stacked against you, and you may be in your darkest period, as well. But I'm here to encourage you to learn to have faith and keep the faith. Believe that you will prevail and be victorious through His grace and mercy.

Keep in mind that when I say, "Have faith and keep the faith," I'm saying this as a man who has gone through a life-threatening accident. I come from my own experience when I tell you to keep the faith and trust.

When something tragic happens to us, we can get caught up in our current circumstances and trials. We get focused on our situation, and get distracted by it, forgetting that there is a greater plan for us.

You just have to trust, believe, and know that it's all going to work out for His good and yours. You may find yourself in uncomfortable, unfamiliar territory at times, and in bad situations—just like when I was in unfamiliar territory, lying in that hospital bed, unable to do anything for myself for the first time in my life.

I had to learn how to trust, believe, and know that it was God's will that was going to get me through this. He was giving me a fresh start and He can give you a fresh start too.

I ask myself whether the tragic, life-threatening accident that happened to me could have possibly been God's will. I wonder if maybe it happened so that I could be an example to others of God's greatness, healing, and restorative power.

I also recently asked myself this question for the first time: *What if all the hard work I put into football, baseball, and basketball…the many hours I spent on the field and on the court, the times I would practice instead of being out having fun…what if it was never about sports at all? What if all my training was God's way of training me to be strong and ready for the bullet that was coming my way one day?*

Think about it. Who would be better equipped to handle a bullet to the head than an athlete?

I may not know the answer to any of these questions until I go home to Heaven. What I do know for sure is this: that you're reading the words of a man who was expected to either die in the operating room, or come out of surgery unable to ever live a normal life again, due to diminished brain functionality.

But my life and yours are worth fighting for, just like I fought to regain functionality while I was in the hospital and afterwards. And, just like I was fighting in the hospital, I'm going to keep fighting for what's next in my life. I know that God had—and has!—a better plan for me. I now realize that it's His will to use my accident for his glory.

I hope and pray that you too will keep fighting. I encourage you to do so.

I could have given up on life and God—but He didn't give up on me. I hope I can be a living, breathing reminder to you that God does not give up on us. He will not give up on you.

Whatever you're going through now and whatever you go through in the future, just know that you can and will survive it. Life will knock you down. When you get knocked down, look up! That's where your help is going to come from.

When you look up, you're letting God know that you trust Him, that you're not staying down, that you're confident that He will help you get back up. That's what I did when I was in the hospital, lying on my back.

As soon as I was able to open my eyes after surgery, I was looking straight up because I knew that was where my help was going to come from.

I'm a winner and so are you. I'm going to win because I'm on the winning team—Team Jesus. I was in God's hands during and after my accident, and every day since then. He has had His hands on me the entire time. God is shaping me, molding me, and building a future where I'll do great and mighty things in His name.

I just have to stay focused and keep pushing and grinding. I'm holding on because I know a change is coming. I'm expecting something great. You too will get a second chance in life, just like God has given me. It's up to you what you do with it.

I'm telling you one thing—I'm going to make the best of this second chance that God has given me. I hope and pray that you do the same.

We are all blessed with different talents. Some of us are blessed with unbelievably special talents, and I'm one of them. I was uniquely created with unbelievably great athletic ability, yet now I'm having to find a way to use these talents in more indirect way. It is quite a transition to switch my mindset away from striving to be a professional football or baseball player.

My mission now is to allow God to guide me into new ways to use the talents He has given me, since I won't be able to use them on the ball field. We have to use the talents that we're blessed with in this second chance we're getting at life and be a blessing to others.

There is a reason God healed my brain sufficiently for me to be able to write this book. (Of course, I did have help from an editor.) And, my brain functionality returned to the point where I could make it through two college semesters of computer science classes, and six months of I.T. classes.) I can't see the exact details right now, but I know that I was created for greatness.

Don't give up on God because He didn't bring you the outcome you wanted Him to. Don't let that kill your faith. There's a greater yes on the other side.

There's a process to everything. As I go through this process and keep getting stronger, my faith keeps getting stronger. It's not over until God says it's over. Just know that you and I are being set up by God to win.

God is not through with me yet. He knows the road I need to take. So, I'm going to allow Him to take the wheel, to lead and guide me. I know that this life I've already lived can't be all there is. God is calling me to something beyond what I can even imagine. My destiny is much bigger and greater than I can even imagine.

I'm going to keep trusting and believing that there's greatness ahead for me. I see my life as a gift and so should you.

Like Brian Courtney Williams sings in his song, *Worth Fighting For, Eyes haven't seen, ears haven't heard all you have planned for me, and nothing can separate me from your love when there's so much more still worth fighting for…*

You haven't seen or heard the last of Gabriel Tuggle. This is just the beginning for me.

Afterword

Yes, God is real. He still performs miracles. I am one of them!

These days, I am in excellent physical condition. I can walk, talk, work, and enjoy life. I even work out four days a week. When I got out of the hospital, I was weak, and could hardly walk or talk. Now I am able to walk and talk, and I am in good physical shape.

A few years after the accident, I even played competitive softball. Unfortunately, I can no longer play football or baseball. There are two reasons for that—the accident and the natural course of aging. But, as I said, I am able to work out four days a week now.

For my workouts, I do flat-bench, incline, and fly presses with dumbbells. One week, I do free weights and the next week, I do the machine circuit. I also take walks around the park near my home. I usually try to walk at a fast pace to get my heart rate up, and sometimes I walk at a normal pace. I mix it up.

I have also regained most of my brain function. I do notice a little bit of a time delay when I'm trying to process something. And I have a minor stutter. Other than those small things, I can speak well. If you heard me speak, you would never guess that I had been shot in the head years earlier, right in the speech center of my brain.

About a year and a half after the accident, I stopped going back for checkups with Dr. Gropper, the neurosurgeon. When he released me from his care, he told me that I was doing great, so I should continue what I was doing. It was clear that my routines were working. He told me that I was and am a miracle.

I couldn't agree more. It is amazing that I'm still here.

*****

I've often heard pastors say that they are chosen with a special calling on their life. I too believe that God created me differently. He designed me for a specific purpose. I believe that I was created to be an overcomer, designed to overcome the extreme challenges I would face after my accident. God created me to be a resilient, relentless, unstoppable, fierce, and fearless overcomer.

I want to tell you now about overcoming a second event that was truly catastrophic. It all started in 1988 around Christmastime—a couple of years before my accident.

It was our family tradition to meet at the home of a different family member every Christmas Eve. This year, we were all going to celebrate at our house. I had something else in mind for the evening—being sexually intimate with my girlfriend for the first time.

My cousin and I had made secret arrangements for me to use his family's house to romance my girlfriend, since everyone was going to be busy at our house, celebrating Christmas Eve.

My girlfriend and I were at my family's celebration for part of the evening, and then we slipped out unnoticed. As you all know, nine times out of ten when you try to sneak around and do something, it comes back to bite you.

It's not that we got caught in the act. We were able to have our intimate interlude. Then, weeks later, we got a little surprise. Actually, it was a big surprise! My girlfriend turned up pregnant.

I had made a big mistake by failing to use protection. That's understandable. As humans, we all make mistakes. As I stated at the beginning, this is not a perfect story as I am not a perfect man.

There I was, this athlete with God-given talent and a promising future, and I had gotten this young lady pregnant. I had no idea how to handle the situation. The one thing I knew for sure was that I was not going to let it keep me from staying focused on my mission to become a professional ball player.

Naturally, my mom and my coaches were very disappointed in me. My mom and my girlfriend's dad even got into a terrible argument over the phone. My girlfriend's parents claimed that I forced my girlfriend to have sex with me. My mom didn't believe that for a minute.

After Mom got off the phone with my girlfriend's dad, she told me what was going on. She said that my girlfriend's parents were convinced that their daughter didn't have sex with *anyone*. That's how they jumped to the conclusion that I must have forced myself on her.

I didn't force myself on her and didn't have to! She knew exactly what she was doing with me. She wanted it to happen as much as I did.

My girlfriend's family told my mom that they didn't want anything to do with me or my family. They didn't want us to have any part in my child's life. As a young man who didn't have a father in his life, I was very hurt by this.

I had been raised to be accountable and responsible. I had taken on and learned about responsibilities at an early age by doing household chores. I didn't want to be irresponsible, the kind of person who would put my child through the same thing my siblings and I had gone through. I didn't want my child to grow up without their father—me!—in their life.

During the pregnancy, the family never reached out to me or my mom. Then, late in the evening on September 19th, 1989, the phone rang. I had already finished football practice, dinner, and homework.

My girlfriend's family called at nine or ten o'clock that night to tell us that my baby had been born that morning. I now had a son named Adrian Bernard. They invited me to come see him.

My girlfriend's brother said, "Let him hold him," but her mother said, "No! Don't you let him touch him!" They held him and let me look at him, but they wouldn't let me hold him.

I saw Adrian only that once when he was an infant. Then when I was in my mid-to-late twenties, I saw him in the neighborhood, running around and playing. He was three or four years old at the time. The only way I knew it was him was that his mom was calling his name.

"What's up, Adrian?" I said.

Instead of answering me directly, he turned to his mom and asked, "Does this man know me?"

She said, "Nope."

When Adrian was old enough to make his own decisions, he reached out to me and began a relationship over the phone. Then, about a month later, he reached out and let me know that he wanted to see me.

I was totally shocked and joyful. I made arrangements with his mother to meet him at the mall, pick him up, and keep him for the weekend. (Adrian's mom was married by then). Thankfully, it wasn't awkward between us. By that time, we had been texting and talking by phone for a while.

Tragically, ten days before his twenty-fourth birthday, my son died in an automobile accident.

I had just had a conversation with Adrian the day before the accident. I was at a friend's house watching a football game when my son called. He had some questions and wanted to talk.

I stepped out of my friend's house, talked to Adrian for a few moments and then said, "Let's talk more later or tomorrow, son." We never got to finish that conversation.

The accident occurred following a terrible argument with his girlfriend. He took the car his grandparents had given him and went out for a drive. Unfortunately, because he was so upset, he was driving recklessly.

He drove around a curve at a speed of somewhere between eighty and a hundred miles per hour. He flipped the car and hit some trees. He lived only a handful of hours and died at the hospital.

I felt devastated and numb when I heard the news. No one wants to bury their child. We had been developing a good solid relationship—and it was cut short suddenly. I only had a relationship with him for five or six years before his death.

Since I had been out of my son's life for so long (through no fault of my own), he had a lot of questions for me. And, we had our difficulties, differences, and arguments. But we were heading in the right direction.

I overcame this terrible tragedy and horrible loss in the same way I overcame my gunshot to the head—through God's grace and mercy and the love and support of friends and loved ones.

In the Bible at Jeremiah 1:5, it states:

Before I formed you in the womb, I knew you. Before you were born, I set you apart; I appointed you as a prophet to the nations.

God knew when he created me that I was going to be an overcomer, an example in this world for believers and nonbelievers alike. He knew that someday He would use me in a mighty and powerful way, to impact lives.

When you have God in your life, you can overcome anything. With God, nothing is impossible. In fact, with God, you can be stronger than a speeding bullet.

About the Author

Gabriel Tuggle faced major obstacles right out of the gate. Despite the challenges he had to overcome, he became an exceptional athlete and made a name for himself throughout his grade school years.

As graduation neared, he was being recruited by top Division 1 schools to play college football and baseball. Before he could ever begin his promising college football and baseball career—a milestone on his way to realizing his dream of playing in the NFL—he was the victim of a tragic gunshot accident.

Tuggle was shot in the head point blank with a .44 caliber gun by a member of a dance group he had joined. His life was interrupted and nearly brought to an end before he could even graduate from high school.

The doctors at the hospital where he was treated fully expected him to either die from his injuries, or be unable to ever live a normal life again, due to diminished brain functionality. Exceeding all expectations, Gabriel summoned the same motivation and drive that molded and shaped him into an elite athlete and used it to recapture 90% of his functionality. He also relied heavily on the healing power of God during his long recuperation.

To be able to live a full life after being shot in the head point blank can only be considered a miracle. Gabriel now has a new mission in life: to use this God-given second chance to be an instrument of God, and a vessel for His message.

"Between my supermom and my entire family who stood by my side and supported me through it all, and the wisdom and guidance given to me by my grandfather who helped raise me, I had a strong foundation that helped me to be an overcomer. But it was God himself who created and built me to be an overcomer. It is my hope that in telling my story of overcoming terrible challenges, I will be able to motivate and inspire others to strive for greater heights of faith and trust in God's healing, grace, and restorative power."

When the author is not working, working out, engaged in worship and prayer, or spending time with his wonderful family and friends, he can often be found watching sports or walking on the nature trails near his home in Atlanta, Georgia.

He believes that with a strong work ethic, the determination to go the extra mile and let nothing stop you, the support of loved ones, and God's guidance, protection, and direction, all things are possible.

About the Author

Imagine training for years to become a professional football or baseball player and knowing that you've got what it takes to make it into the NFL or MLB. You're young, strong, quick, and blessed with athletic prowess and abilities that make your coaches and fellow teammates sit up and take notice. You perfect your skills and your game while the other kids are out enjoying recreational time. The brass ring is within reach. Soon, your dream will come true. You are on your way to fulfilling your mission in life. You smile, envisioning how good it will feel to make your mark in the record books as one of the greatest football or baseball players in history. At last, you will be in a position to provide your mother with the kind of life she deserves.

Then, a single joking remark made to the wrong person at the wrong time shatters your dream. Everything you've worked toward dies in an instant—but miraculously, you live. This is the story of a young man who discovers that he is stronger than a bullet. In these pages, you will read about his remarkable journey from victim to victor, and the incredible new vision and mission he has been given by God for his future.

CPSIA information can be obtained
at www.ICGtesting.com
Printed in the USA
JSHW060048201222
35208JS00001BA/47